30 years in my trade and I have had the pleasure of meeting so many lovely people. As a man of strong principles, I soon decided to work for myself. I'm an experienced and skilled kitchen fitter, thriving on completely satisfied customers. However, nothing annoys me more than trivial complaints when there are so many in the world with so little! As an optimist in life, I always try to focus on what I have, not what I don't; always trying to see the good in others and aspiring to help others whenever I can.

Who knows what I'll do next!

I would like to dedicate this book to my great friend Neil Heming, whom we sadly lost in October 2020 after a long battle with cancer. He was an inspiring guy and a true lifelong friend. He had amazing passion and love for the great outdoors and was simply my rock during the last gruelling days of my challenge!

Brian Morgan

# TO HELL AND BACK FOR CHARITY!

AUSTIN MACAULEY PUBLISHERS™

LONDON • CAMBRIDGE • NEW YORK • SHARJAH

A CIP catalogue record for this title is available from the British Library.

ISBN 9781528985239 (Paperback)
ISBN 9781528985246 (ePub e-book)

www.austinmacauley.com

First Published 2023
Austin Macauley Publishers Ltd®
1 Canada Square
Canary Wharf
London
E14 5AA

# Chapter 1
# I Have an Idea!

Where do we start? I've never written a book before and to be quite frank, I've never read that many either. Mind, that's me throwing myself into the deep end again and hoping something decent comes out the other side. Just another challenge I guess, fastest way of learning. Yes, we're going to make a few mistakes I guess but that's life.

It's all the things that we do wrong in life that somehow builds a strong platform for getting things right. The irony is that by the time we may have worked it all out and gotten it all right, it's probably all over! How many people do you know spend years getting their home just perfect and then when it's finally done, they move on; well, there's a thought!

I have learnt a lot about myself recently, mind learnt a lot about others, far more than I was expecting to be honest. Since I left school, I've spent years dealing with the public. One of the nicest parts of my job as a kitchen fitter has been that you spend a week in somebody's house, get to know people on a little more personal level than just hello, goodbye on the street and then move on before overstaying your welcome.

It's taught me how to adapt and to get on with people of all walks of life. The one big thing it has taught me over the years is just how incredibly different we all are in the way we think, the things we enjoy doing, how we value different things in life and most interestingly, how we all interact with others.

I'd say that has put me in good stead for the negative side of life. The experience I have gained over the years and the acceptance of others regardless to their differences, no doubt helped me cope with any negative comments and emotional put downs I was about to receive regards to my challenge.

Fortunately for every one of these, I found there's always someone around the next corner so grateful for what you are doing and they're always a much bigger person than the last in my eyes.

I'm going to try my best to not offend and I'm going to sincerely apologise now if I do. We are all different and I understand that. I guess the world would be a much less colourful place if we weren't. After all, it's the bad people in life that make the good people shine out! If only they realised that, some would probably be quite upset about it!

Oh and by the way, if you see a few mistakes through the book, they're probably not mistakes. It's just me saying it as it is. I wasn't born with a silver spoon in my mouth and no money in the world would ever change that. Now there's another thing I could waffle on about, so I'm going to stop myself there. Let's get on with the book.

It must have been back some time last year, around about Autumn half term time, that I first had this thought in my head to do something for charity. So, Autumn 2015. I really don't know where it came from or what even inspired me to be honest, it could of course be the inspiration of many things that just came to bursting point, I really don't know.

I guess it's all to do with the subconscious mind. Now, I'm not religious at all but it was as if a big hand reached down, took me up into the clouds, someone had had a good talking to me, then placed me back down on earth.

I suddenly went from having no thought at all about it to having this huge urge in my mind that had already decided that I was definitely doing it. Strangest thing was at this stage, I didn't even know what I was doing, other than the word WALK was also screaming out at me.

So, the seed had been planted in my mind but bear in mind at this stage I had no idea when I was walking, where I was walking or how far or even if I was really going ahead with the whole idea. Considering this in my own mind of course and I hadn't even yet mentioned it to my own family.

Without my wife's blessing, this would have been a real stumbling block for the whole thing. I like to think I have a real close relationship with my family and a whole lot of respect for my wife, more than she probably realises, if she would have said no, the whole challenge would have been scuppered.

I'm going to stay as close to the facts as I possibly can. There are a few bits here and there that are now vague memories in my head but I'm going to piece them together as best as I can. Fortunately, there are also a huge amount of very vivid images in my head too!

Of course, had I have known at the time I was going to write a book; I would have kept more notes. It wasn't in fact until about my third or fourth day or more of walking that I first had any thought of writing. I do wonder sometimes if my brain's wired a bit differently to most.

I seem to have gone through life doing things on the spur of the moment, madness ideas. Do you ever meet people that seem to have a story about everything? Well, that's often me but the thing is they are not made up! I've seen some of the strangest things happen and some of the strangest of coincidences.

Anyway, now I knew my wife was ok with this, it was like giving me the green light to go and I couldn't see anything whatsoever standing in my way. Nothing was going to hold me back, it was just a case of choosing the right paths, geographically and remaining very positive.

Positive thinking is something I can be very good at; I would certainly call myself an optimist. It's extremely rare for me to be pessimistic about anything, life's too short!

My next mission I think was to spill the beans a little, slightly expose my mind but with caution at this stage. Thinking back now, I think there were two real motives battling with each other in my little head. One was to reveal my intentions, not just to see the reaction of others but almost like building a wall behind me of no return.

Once I had told someone that I was going to do it, it sort of made it final. There was no turning back without consequences, that being consequences I could mentally deal with, with not too much shame upon myself of failing before I'd started, so just a select few at this stage.

The other thought was to not say too much yet as I hadn't even checked out a route to see if it was even possible to do this whole crazy thing. So, caution battles madness once again. Some people in life seem to have mad ideas that turn out to be ingenious. I just seem to have mad ideas that turn out be, well just mad ideas!

Looking back now, it must have been early autumn last year when I first thought about doing this walk. I just traced back on my phone to a conversation I had, by text of course as you do nowadays, to a very good friend of mine. One of the very first people I had mentioned anything to.

If there was ever anyone who may have been interested in coming along with me, it was me old mate Edd. Well, I say Edd but his real name's Neil Heming; been calling him Edd for so many years now, can't even remember why! Anyway, the conversation was right at the end of October and went a bit like this:

*"Planning a charity walk for next spring, approx. 334 miles, are you interested?"*

Edd: *"Alright geezer, long time no see. Yes, I'd be up for a long-distance walk. Out at the mo., so I'll call later."*

So that was really cool, he sounded really keen, I knew if anybody would be interested it would be him, bit of an outdoor man himself. Thought I'd send him back a bit more information, so I text back:

*"Sounds cool, talk to you soon; was planning St Paul's Cathedral to Land's End!"*

Took all of about five minutes to get back a reply:

Edd: *"That's a monster trip m8, what timescale are you thinking?"*

I replied:

*"Was planning 12 days?"*

Edd: *"That's tough, about 28 miles a day!"*

So, he's done the maths and had a prompt reality check, and I could sense the hesitation approaching. So then comes the typical male to male banter:

*"Bottling out already?"*

He had to think about this one, a full six minute passed before his reply. Of course, he couldn't let it lie on that!

Edd: *"No mate, just being realistic, let's see how macho you are when you got a blister the size of a golf ball!"*

Of course, I couldn't resist but replied back myself even knowing there was probably a lot of sensibleness in what he was actually saying, so I kept the conversation light and turned to our humorous side and of course, a boost of masculinity as man mates do.

*"Wow, that's half the size of me nuts!"*

That was the last of our conversation for a while. I'm pretty sure I'd done a good job of enticing him along with me and scaring him off, all in the space of about 20 minutes.

I came up with the idea of walking from St Paul's Cathedral in London, all the way down to Land's End in Cornwall. If I was going to do something worthy of collecting money for charity, it had to be some kind of a challenge. It had to be something that stood out and caught people's attention in some way. It also had to be practical, so as I could travel to the start point with ease and home again without too much bother or expense involved.

Land's End seemed an obvious place to walk to. Everybody seems to involve Land's End, but most seem to use it as a starting point. I wanted to use it as my destination. My start point also needed to be iconic in some way.

London seemed to be a good choice as a start but London's such a huge place I needed something more specific. St Paul's Cathedral seemed to fit perfectly, right in the heart of London, quite central in fact and a famous landmark.

Once a route was established, timing was my next issue. Well, when I say route established, at this point of course the route was very vague indeed, London to Land's End, somehow! Timing was going to be an issue for me. I'm self-employed, the only source of income for my family and not exactly rolling in cash to be able to take a sustained period of time out of work.

Of course, getting the balance right here was of major importance to us. Too long off work was going to cost me, too short a period allowed to cover the ground could become impractical and of course, lead to a head on collision with failure.

I also had this idea in my head to see if it was at all possible to plan a route between St Paul's in London and Land's End, stopping at Premier Inn and nowhere else, after all Premier Inn guarantees you a good night sleep and breakfast, enough to set you up for any day's work or play or walk in my case.

I've been stopping in Premier Inn for years and in my experience, they have been very good at delivering this and very consistent wherever you stay. In the back of my mind, I was going to write to Premier Inn and see if they would get behind me in some way, after all this was for charity and seemed like a good bit of PR for them, to be able to walk from London to Land's End using no more than just their Inns. We'll talk about this later.

My initial planning of the route was to plot out in rough on a map, every Inn between London and Land's End. My next task was to collate as much information as I could recording distances from Inn to Inn. Most of the route then fell in place with a few options here and there with my biggest stumbling block being between Salisbury and Yeovil.

The distance here between them just seemed far too great to be practical in a day, even for my crazy standards, so I looked at pulling slightly off course by throwing in Frome. So, it was going to cost me a few extra miles, but failure wasn't an option, it just had to work.

My route was now planned in rough on a scrap piece of paper, something to work with at least. A 13-day route would have made life a bit more comfortable, not that I'm superstitious at all but it just didn't have the same appeal to me as 12 days, as in a dozen.

14 days would have been even easier but then we'd have been starting to stretch it out a bit too much. It just had to be a challenge and had to be kept as short as practically possible.

My next communication with Edd was in December. Met up with him on mutual turf in Reading. I live in Newbury, and he lives in Burham, Slough. It's not often we get together these days to be honest, we've stayed good mates for years and years, went to school together.

As the years go by you grow up, have a family and going out for a drink has become a bit more of a rare occasion. Besides we also live in different towns now but nevertheless have always remained close friends. I think if I remember correctly, I contacted him a week before we met up.

It was on a Saturday, not too late in the day, now we really are showing our age, however on the practical side we both needed to catch a train back home.

I took with me the scrap piece of paper outlining my walk, route and distances between places and kept a photocopy for my own reference. We didn't mention the walk at all for a while. He almost seemed a little bit reluctant to get involved. I don't think it was just the distance that was putting him off but more the nature of the whole thing.

His idea of a nice walk was sweeping through the countryside at a casual to moderate pace, taking in the views, the wild country air, with the odd acquaintance with a few refreshment houses along the way if you know what I mean. Well, I must say, sounds absolutely perfect to me but the problem was that it couldn't have been more different than the walk I had planned.

Take away the word leisure and pleasure and take away the country air and replace it with traffic fumes and noise and that pretty much sums up a large proportion of my route. This was more of a march of stamina and endurance and purely for the purpose of trying to raise as much money as possible for a great cause.

I could fully understand the attraction or lack of it rather. I think I was definitely losing his interest. I think he knows me well enough or should do to know that when I've made my mind up about something I am not easily dissuaded. If I was going to do this complete walk on my Jack Jones, so be it, that's how it would be.

My parents were fingers crossed hoping my mate would come on board, so I didn't say too much about things at this point, I didn't want to disappoint them. I think we left things with Edd that maybe we could look at an alternative route, but I knew that that would take a lot of work and was unlikely to happen in reality.

This was my idea, my walk, my route, my planning and my way! I'd like to think that I'm not a selfish person in life and to be quite frank can be very diplomatic at times when I need to be but this was my idea, crazy as it was but that's just me!

I think it was Christmas that year when I stumbled upon a pair of boots fit for the job. Well in fact I know it was and when I say I stumbled, I mean I certainly wasn't out searching for a pair at the time.

It was sometime over the Christmas festive period; I can't remember now which day, but it was one of those cheap discount stores that just happened to be open while browsing round a small town in Devon.

Running up to Christmas that year, I really had been working my nuts off as usual and I was completely knackered. To be quite honest I'm not really a Christmas fan anyway so it didn't take a lot of self-persuading to convince myself that a break away for the festive period was on the cards. Funny enough I didn't even set out to go to North Devon.

Fancied Pembrokeshire, Southwest Wales, a nice little property somewhere, miles away from all the hustle and bustle, some nice sea air, a few nice idyllic coastal paths and some valuable family time! Sounded great to me but Pembrokeshire it wasn't to be, just couldn't find the right property, however we are talking quite last minute for a booking, so choice was fairly limited.

The fact that it was winter, short days, long evenings, we would be spending more time in than out, so the right property was all important to us. Failing this, my search widened with property at top of the list and location taking second priority and we ended up in North Devon.

Never stopped in North Devon before so that was quite exciting, a new area to explore. Always seem to bypass Devon and moved on to Cornwall. What a cracking property it turned out to be. An old refurbished or more accurately described, a recently rebuilt round house set in the middle of a 300acre sheep farm. The owners were also fantastic, would love to go back there one day for a second visit.

Whoops! I do feel we're drifting off the subject a bit. So, there we were browsing round this cheap shop, when there on the shelf was this pair of boots shining out at me and in a weird way somehow calling out to me. There they were sitting on the shelf with just a small display of other boots around them.

Obviously end of line, misshaped, knocked off or faulty in some way shape or form. I walked around a couple of times with this quiet nagging in the back of my mind, *'going to need a pair of boots if I do this charity walk, I mean WHEN I do it'*. Down to about £25 seemed too good to be true for the way they presented themselves.

Temptation got to the better of me and before I knew it there I was trying a pair on. Couldn't believe my luck, only had a few pairs on the shelf and just happened to have my size. Slipped my foot in and fitted like a glove. For a moment I felt like a male version of Cinderella.

Finding a pair of boots that ticked all the right boxes without costing me an arm and a leg was always going to be a task and half but suddenly seemed so simply accomplished. The padding around the ankles was just superb, it was like buying an engine that had already been run in.

I'm guessing that younger people probably wouldn't know what I meant by that. I was specifically after a pair of boots as opposed to trainers to eliminate or reduce the chance of twisting an ankle, walking long distance over uneven ground. So, in the basket they went.

At the end of the day what had I lost, if I didn't end up using them for my walk, I picked myself up a decent pair of walking boots for £25. Gets to the till, cashier zapped away, and they came up I think about £32, something to do with them being a bigger size apparently.

Not to worry, £32 still seemed to be a bargain. So, there you go, I'm now one step closer to doing my walk and if I had some kind of made-up mad fandangle walk meter machine, the needle would have just raised a tad further from the base.

Christmas passed plus a few months, nothing really progressed much to be honest, it seemed quite a way off, but time has a way of creeping up on you, so it was never far from my thoughts. A proper route had to be set in concrete and of course I had to make a final decision on what charity I wanted to raise funds for.

I had a good idea where we were going with that, as I'd already made my mind up it was going to be for some kind of children's charity. I must admit this was one area where I felt a little uneasy, all the effort I was about to put in and which charity do I trust?

I don't mean to sound distrusting but you are always cautious of charities out there that make themselves out to be so caring and wonderful but when you take a deeper look inside, you discover it's a very small amount that actually has a direct effect.

The rest helps line the pockets of some very greedy unscrupulous people. So, I started to look at some children's charities, even downloaded some facts and figures to get an idea of how some so-called do-gooders preformed. I finally decided it would be '*Make a Wish UK*'.

There were several reasons for my choice. The three main reasons were, it's specifically for children and young adults, it's a general charity when it comes to conditions, I know a large proportion is different types of cancers, but it doesn't specify just one particular illness, plus also it's a nationally recognised charity so hopefully this would be helpful in raising funds.

'*Make a Wish UK*' really is a fantastic charity as it aims to enrich the lives of children and young adults suffering from life threatening conditions. It allows children to do things that would otherwise not be possible, a short time away from hospital treatment and given the chance to fulfil their dreams.

Not only does this wonderful charity help make these dreams come true but also in doing so, creates priceless memories for so many young people, irreplaceable to family members when tragically and inevitably some of these children pass away.

So, I made contact with '*Make a Wish*', looked up their contact details on the net and gave them a call. There are lots of ways you can help this charity, many organised events too but I wanted to do my own thing.

I had a short conversation with one of their members of staff and got myself registered with them. They sent me a few useful links i.e., some manual letter headed sponsor sheets, a letter of authority to say they were accepting me as an honest volunteer for their cause and a link to set up a just giving site via the web.

I was sort of led to believe that everybody nowadays donates online which sounded great to me as I would be able to raise money without any cash passing through my hands. As it turned out, it didn't quite pan out totally this way, as we'll talk about later.

I must also admit I was a little bit sceptical about being able to set up my just giving page, but I just followed the prompts, and it was all quite simple really. First thing I did was to donate a very small amount myself just to see that it was all working and of course it gave me great feeling of satisfaction to lift it off the ground even if it was from my own pocket.

Suddenly made it all feel a bit more real having somewhere where people could donate which I thought would be so easy. Unfortunately, I found out there are more people out there that are reluctant to donate through the internet than I first thought!

So now I had a just giving site set up and some sponsor forms, my thoughts then turned to how to promote this whole thing. Doing the actual event is one thing but unless I had people to sponsor me then it was all a bit of a pointless exercise.

I felt if I was going to be asking people to donate then I needed some way of presenting the facts of what I was doing, so I set about making a poster like information sheet that had a quick impact diagram of my walk. I produced a map of South England, approximately to scale and I plotted on all my stops from London to Land's End. On this sheet, I also had the total miles I was covering and the dates I was intending to walk.

Fixing a date for the walk had to be done with a bit of careful planning in mind. It needed to be done when daylight hours were at an advantage to me so somewhere around June seemed favourable. Also, to be considered was the weather.

Although impossible to predict, July was ruled out for the fact it can get quite hot, stop laughing it happens now and again in England, which of course could be a problem with dehydration and having to carry so much water. Too early in the year and I would have to carry too much heavy clothing.

You have to remember this was going to be a completely unaided walk, no doctors or physios following me round or a taxi for when I'd had enough like you see when some of these stars do their bit, not that we're not still grateful to them. I'd be carrying a full load for nearly two weeks and when the going got tough it would be just a case of keep going to till you reached your destination.

Anyway, so I got this sheet laminated and alongside this I had another sheet which showed a table of all the individual miles I was doing per day. It was about 335 miles in 12 days which averaged out about 28 miles a day. My shortest stretch was 19.5 miles and my longest about 35.6 miles. I must admit, it was beginning to sound like a daunting task just thinking about it!

Prior to producing this information, I had been spreading the word a bit more to people I knew and the response I was getting was really encouraging. Through many different sources I knew many different people and if only half of then helped out I felt confident that I could easily raise a decent amount of cash.

There were friends through my job, clients, tradesmen, shops that I used on a regular basis, karate, neighbours, family, etc. Now armed with a bit more information I felt ready to approach a lot more of them.

I needed to get on and write to Premier Inn as I needed to get these dates booked. If I left it all too late, just one location fully booked could throw a spanner in the works for the whole thing! So, I wrote to Premier Inn explaining what I was about to do, in the hope that I would get some kind of a response back from them.

To be honest I thought that this could be a good bit of PR for them stopping at their Inns and only their Inns all the way from London to Land's End, most people wouldn't even realise that could be done.

As well, I was hoping that they could help me out with the cost in some way as this was going to cost me a few quid out of my own pocket as I was looking for 12 nights and during the week too when some were quite pricey. I did of course prepare myself for the fact that I may end up paying full fare for the whole lot but forever optimistic as I am, I carried on with my plans regardless.

You do hear about people taking their expenses out of the money they have raised but this was certainly not going to happen. I was hoping to raise at least £5000 pound which didn't mean raising £6000 then scooping off £1000 to cover my expenses.

I wanted 100% of all proceeds to go direct to the charity. You do hear about people having a bit of a jolly for themselves doing activities and things and making out it was all for charity, well that certainly wasn't going to be the case here. On 5 March 2016, I wrote a letter and sent it recorded to The Managing Director at Premier Inn headquarters.

# Chapter 2
# Training

Coincidently, my son Matthew was given the opportunity to take part in a walking challenge with his school this year. It's called Ten Tours and takes place in Dartmoor. As far as I'm aware, it's an annual event which is run by the MOD and caters for thousands of young participants every year.

The school then have to take all willing volunteers through a course of training walks as they are eventually to be left alone in small groups in the middle of Dartmoor with no adult supervision. So of course, the school have to be satisfied they have some good basic skills such as good map reading skills, stamina and etc. and are able to work well as a team together with a few basic survival skills.

Of course, nowadays with modern technology I believe they all carry tracking devices, which is a great asset for peace of mind for all. The idea is that they gradually illuminate the weakest so as to choose the final candidates from the few remaining strongest competitors.

I was sure Matthew had a good chance of being selected as they seemed to have a lack of volunteers this year. Mind he still had to prove himself worthy. He also happened to be one of the only pupils that had attended every training course!

Seeing him training made me think a bit more about my own training. I started to wonder if I could join the school on one of their training sessions for my own benefit. Unfortunately, most of the walks were not circular and I found myself having to drive round to various locations to collect him.

Their last training walk however, which happened to be about 20k if I remember rightly and happened to be a circular walk, starting and finishing at the same location over in Hungerford. This sounded like a great opportunity for me, so on his last but one walk I had a plan when picking him up.

I would take the opportunity to ask if I could gate crash his last walk. I must say his teacher seemed quite taken back that a parent had made such a request as it would seem that at that age, 15 by the way, parents and children, young adults, do everything they can, not to be together, especially when it comes to anything to do with school.

I understood where she was coming from, but I'd say I've a very close relationship with the boys and very much value the time we spend together. Anyway, after getting over the initial shock, she couldn't see any real problem with this but suggested that I wrote some official kind of note as a formal request. I did just that!

On the day of the walk, we all met up at a location on Hungerford Common. I packed a light rucksack, a damn site lighter than the load all the young lads were having to carry. For training purposes, all pupils were made to carry a minimum amount so as to prepare for the real event.

Surely this would be a piece of cake for me! There were two groups of lads. The older years were training for a longer walk. 13th March it was if I remember rightly, as I said I'm going to do my best to remember all the facts. I've had to do a fair bit of detective work to get some dates in order of when I done what and where, even down to tracing back a receipt to a garage I visited on one of my walks to be able to pinpoint the date of that particular walk.

Anyway, back to Hungerford and there we were all assembled in this small gravel carpark about to embark on this great country stroll or hike rather. Half surprisingly to me, it was soon suggested that I was to be appointed to the group with the older lads.

I say half surprisingly because I'm sure I got a slight sense of this when Matt's teacher had spoken to me on the phone prior to this, in response to my official note of request. I do believe it something to do with keeping parents and pupils apart, some kind of school policy apparently.

I do sort of understand the reasoning behind this so after making my protest, I kept in mind to keep well away from Matt the vast majority of the time. From a logical point of view, for me it seemed crazy that I was going to end up back at our meeting point at a totally different time to the younger lads, only to be standing around waiting for them to finish.

Plus of course, I would be walking along with a complete group of strangers with not one single person I knew, not even by face. I may well have walked off in a different direction on my own through the countryside and walked a different day entirely.

The walk went well, had a light chat with most people as you do, just passing the time of day. Even had a chat with some of the students whilst of course doing my best to keep clear of Matt, which seemed strange but for his own benefit. We seemed to get off at a great pace, almost like a march, which was great for me, the exact sort of training I needed.

If I was going to walk 30 something miles a day, then pace was all so important. The average walking pace is apparently 3 miles/hour or so I'm led to believe. You then need to add extra time on to that for any breaks, map reading, inclinations, carrying luggage, etc.

So, you do the maths, I could be in for some very long days if I don't keep up a decent pace. As the hours went by, our pace gradually decreased, and our finishing time seemed to be gradually pushing later and later. The lads were taking it in turn to map read so as to be sure they were all competent at the skill.

With the sheer distance I would be covering, keeping map reading time to a minimum would be crucial. This was one of the major reasons why I was planning to walk using major routes only and not aiming to cut across the land using country paths and trails. Of course, walking alone has its perils too, as you don't want to have an accident on a country path and lay unnoticed for hours or even days.

One of the lads sustained some kind of muscular injury during the walk which was slowing us all up a bit. I did offer to relieve him of his heavy bag but for training purposes, this was forbidden. The other lads had to muscle in and show their support, which I could understand from a training point of view as, if they were to be alone in the middle of Dartmoor, they would all have to be working as a team and helping each other.

The organisers didn't want to cause the lad any real injury, so they called through and arranged a pickup at the next convenient point. There was a school minibus never too far away just as a backup in the event of any unforeseen circumstances. The rest of us pressed on to the finish.

Knowing that the lads had proved themselves today, backup was called, and we finished the last few kilometres in the minibus. I must admit most of them were looking a bit worn out and although I felt ok myself, I was starting to feel a bit of a stiffness in my groins on both sides during the latter part of the walk.

By the time I'd driven home and started to relax, I could really feel my groins aching. It felt as though I had strained something somewhere. I was so glad to have done that walk that day as it taught me a real valuable lesson. It was the furthest I had walked for a few years, and it made me realise just how important it was to get a few more hours training in.

It sounds so easy, walking doesn't it but when it's prolonged and persistent, it puts more strain on you than you realise, especially when carrying a load as well. So, this was a great wakeup call for me to do more training but at the same time I was concerned as how I was going to find the spare time to do it. After all, how do you prepare for that sort of distance other than putting in similar hours of training? My legs were stiff for a few days then gradually eased up.

A few days later, 16$^{th}$ March, and I had a bit of spare time off work. Hadn't heard a sausage back from Premier Inn and was thinking it was time to get these rooms booked up. I'd been checking availability on the web and discovered that one particular location was already fully booked on the date I required.

Fortunately, this was one of the only locations that had an alternative Inn close by, which was only going to add a very small distance to the overall walk and change the route only slightly. It was an Inn down near Newquay. Any other discrepancy could have caused a major problem.

Before I booked, I thought I'd have one last pop at talking to them. I called them up with an ever-optimistic mind but got nowhere. They suggested that I call round the individual branches and see what they could do but they were really just sending me round in circles, I eventually gave up. I was once told that Premier Inn weren't a very charitable company, and it would appear they may be right.

I couldn't afford to delay booking any longer, so I got straight onto the web and booked up all twelve nights. I was staying in London the night before I started my walk so was expecting to pay a few quid due to its location but that wasn't the only expensive one I can tell you. The only night I hadn't booked up yet was final night down at Land's End Hotel.

So, all now booked up, a few paid for now, the rest to be paid for later. It all seemed a bit more real now it was booked. I felt a bit more confident spreading the word as I was not just emotionally committed but financially as well now.

You just don't realise what's involved in organising something like this. It wasn't just 12 days out of my life but an enormous commitment of time and effort to get it all to work and I'd only just scratched the surface.

After the last walk I'd done and the realisation that my body needed to be pushed a bit to prepare it for this gruelling challenge ahead, my thoughts right now were on training. The reaction I was getting from people seemed to be chiefly about the training and of course the amount of it I must be doing or not, well those that actually got what I was doing.

I must say there were a few out there that really didn't get it at all, probably the ones where the furthest they'd ever walked was from their house to their car door! I really did need to do a bit more training as so far, I'd only done the one walk.

On the 20th of March, I did my second training walk. Not wanting to walk too far and preferring not to walk back the same way, I decided to get a train from Newbury to Great Bedwyn and then walk home from there. I can't remember the exact distance, but I think it was about 13 miles.

The one thing that had been bugging me, had been knowing that if I kept the same pace as the overall pace we did on the school walk, then crap, we had a problem, there simply wouldn't be enough hours in a day to complete the distances I was trying to achieve.

The full purpose of this next walk was to set myself some kind of pacemaker mark, to satisfy in my own mind I was capable of achieving the speed I needed to set. I knew there would be large parts of this walk with no proper footpaths, and I couldn't think of a worse road than the A4 from the other side of Hungerford all the way through to Newbury. Long, very, very straight and very boring.

This of course was all part of the training, miles of open road ahead of us, no one to talk to bar the fence and the odd gatepost, all part of the psychology. There's no better training for anything like the real thing.

I set out early that Sunday morning, small rucksack on back with essential supplies, to catch the early morning train to Bedwyn. It was a lovely fine day as far as I remember with your typical chill in the air for that time of year.

Wasn't on my own in the end, Matt decided to join me for support, which was nice of him, so not quite the same psychological training on this one as I thought but I was pretty sure that the sheer boredom of this one would put him right off doing any more. Never caught a train to Bedwyn in my life, probably never will again. Also seemed a bit strange getting a train one way only.

Train arrived bang on time like they do, good old British Rail, no I'm not being sarcastic it did actually arrive on schedule! We arrived at Bedwyn and hastily disembarked, quickly got our bearings and clocked the time. From now on, we were walking against the clock.

I had taken my satnav with us from the car which was great cause not only did it guide us all the way home, first part of the journey being country lanes but also gave us an estimated time of arrival by foot. So, in theory, this was our worst-case scenario.

Didn't get too far before I realised that I'd unfortunately left my walking stick behind somewhere. My first thoughts were that I'd left it on the train but on thinking again, we were both sure that we'd left nothing behind when we got off. No, what an absolute idiot I was, I'd left my stick on the platform at Newbury Station.

I must admit I was gutted, not for the fact I had no stick to carry me home, but it wasn't just any old stick. To me it was almost irreplaceable. It may well of started its life as a common old broom handle but some years back with a bit of careful doctoring, sanding and shaping, I turned that old broom handle into what is now my favourite walking stick.

It was a few years back; I can tell you. Years ago, when the boys were a lot younger, we were off to the Lake District in Cumbria and I made four sticks, two long ones and two short ones, all totally different designs. Of course, the two shorter ones are of no use to any of us now, I mean the boys are as tall as me now, maybe even taller.

I just hoped that stick would still be there on the platform when I returned. After all, it was Newbury we were talking about, more chance of it being handed in than stolen, well at least I would like to think!

So, on we pressed. Still bugging me slightly, all I could do was call the wife and see if she could get in touch with the station to look after my stick till, I got there. I remembered now standing it next to the wall where we were sitting, waiting for the train to arrive.

On we marched keeping up a fair pace. Quite a pleasant start on the country lanes, very peaceful bar the odd vehicle and quite scenic too. I still remember a farmer out nice and early ploughing his fields as we drew ever closer to the A4.

Reached the A4, turned right and headed east, from now on we were to follow this road all the way back. It's a fairly straight road by large so there were times when the way ahead appeared endless but with a steady pace all was to be conquered.

You find yourself setting small goals like the next big tree ahead or lamp post or next bend in the road. We were gradually bit by bit getting ahead of our time, which was great as I was thinking if we could gain some time to stop, we could stop and still remain on our desired time schedule.

Shortly before arriving in Hungerford, I remember passing some laddies. They were out collecting litter along the roadside, part of some litter collecting awareness day or week or something like that. What a fantastic job they were doing. The amount of litter we had passed on the way along such a short stretch of road we had done was quite frankly disgusting.

I don't think carrier bags sprung to mind but more like a pull along skip. I think we've come to a point in this country where people really do need educating on how to look after the environment around them and the importance of it. Anyway, as we passed, we had a brief conversation. When I say brief, it was very brief.

It was a shame because you could tell they wanted to chat. I would have usually been happy to chat, but the time was ticking. It's a shame really because this was exactly how it was going to be when I was to do the walk for real, with time constantly against me every minute chatting would be valuable time lost for walking.

We passed through Hungerford and started thinking about taking a rest somewhere, grabbing a quick bite and rehydrating. We were over halfway and both beginning to feel a little peckish and dehydrated. Stopping along the roadside is not always that simple, you can sometimes walk for miles just to find somewhere convenient to perch yourself.

If I remember rightly, I think we found a crumbly old wall to sit on. It is sometimes easy to walk too far without sufficient breaks and push your body resources further than you should as I found out later.

We didn't stop for long, I think between five and ten minutes in all, just enough time for a quick feed and a fair drink, get some goodness back into the system and rehydrate the fluids. Off we marched again. For some reason, the satnav seemed to keep fluctuating with the estimated time of arrival but overall, we knew that if we kept up pushing the pace, we were well on track for a good time back.

My youngest son Dan had a football match that afternoon and I told my wife we'd be back in time, so no pressure! I remember a big juggernaut passing us along the way home and honking his horn. We'd seen him pass earlier and I can only guess he'd been and delivered his load somewhere in Newbury and was amazed how much ground we had covered when he spotted us on his way back. Of course, I had Matt with me plus I was wearing a charity t-shirt.

We really had been pushing the pace. When we arrived back home, I think we were a couple of decimal points either just over or just under the 4 mile/hour speed, inclusive of our breaks. This was fantastic as it gave me the confidence that I could handle this pace if I needed to. I couldn't imagine that you would want to keep that pace up all day, but I was also thinking that if I trained at that pace, it would put me in good stead for the task ahead.

I must say I had no problems with the muscles this time so that was promising, the only thing I had was a few blisters or almost blisters. I'd say just a bit sore in places around the toes and heels.

Made it to football with Dan ok. Was chatting away with one of the other parents there about the walk we'd just done and one chap I knew was well impressed with our pace, fit lad as well. I still remember him saying.

*"Wow, that's good! That's only an hour longer than me doing the Reading half marathon."* Did also manage to shoot down to the station and see if my stick was still there and all was well, there it was across the platform, sitting right where I'd left it.

A few more weeks passed, no more training, so I was itching to get back out again for another walk. Time was ticking by June seemed ever nearer and well it was another four weeks in fact when I got round to my next walk. The big problem was trying to keep work going, people often don't realise the hours of commitment when you're self-employed.

It was tough trying to find time for training and also time for promoting this whole thing so as to actually raise some funds, after all, that's what it was all about. Then of course after all this there was some all-important family time to squeeze in. I must admit my family were very supportive of me during that time.

I didn't quite realise just how much precious time would be swallowed up when I took on this challenge. I guess the sacrifices my family had to make I'd never really considered properly but nevertheless, I was chuffed with their patience and tolerance and above all this, could even sense a feeling of pride in what I was doing.

On Sunday 17th April, I set off on my next training walk. As I was saying, I'd barely seen my wife and the boys all week and there I was, Sunday morning off work and off on my tod walking again. Matt didn't join me on this one, I think the novelty had worn off, I wasn't surprised.

Checked the weather the night before, it was going to be mainly dry again. To be quite honest it really wouldn't have bothered me if it had been tipping down, after all when I was to do the real thing, I wouldn't be able to pick and choose what days to walk so I was inevitably going to get a good soaking at some point. The chances of escaping rain through Devon and Cornwall would certainly be remote.

Set myself up this morning on a circular route, this way I wouldn't have to worry about getting public transport anywhere, so more flexible start time and cheaper. Can't remember the exact miles, think it was similar to the last but I do remember working out the exact time it would take me if I were to keep up the 4 miles/hour pace.

Playing mind games on myself, I clocked the time on my phone when I set off and didn't look at the time again until I was back on my drive. It was another football day for Dan so again I had to be back by a certain time.

Set off from the house at a brisk pace. I remember again feeling that fresh morning air, after all it was still quite early in the year. I wore two pairs of socks this time to try to combat those sore feet, a decent pair of purpose made walking socks and a thin pair as well. The idea was partly for comfort as well as providing some kind of friction barrier at the same time.

Reach Newbury High Street in no time at all and headed south out of the town. I wasn't exactly expecting to see that many people around on that time on a Sunday morning but surprisingly there were quite a few. A typical Sunday morning always seems to be a slower than normal start, then seems to burst into life halfway through the morning.

It wasn't until I was right up through the town and up past St Gabriel's School that I actually felt like I was getting anywhere, after all up until there I'd walked all those paths before, sometimes too often. I remember passing the tip as they were just opening up with a queue already starting to build down the road. You know those people that just have to be there first at the front of the queue.

Instead of waiting in a queue for 15mins, they'd rather spend 30mins waiting for the gates to open. You may laugh but that's just how stupid some people are. Then of course, there's the people that get up at the crack of dawn, race around doing all there chores as quickly as they can, only to get back home and wonder what to do with themselves for the rest of the day.

Down towards the Swan, if it's still call that, turned left at the roundabout heading towards Basingstoke. I was only walking so far down here then chucking another left and coming right round the edges of Greenham Common and heading back into Thatcham, via the railway crossing before heading home.

It was when I left the main road that the paths became a little more challenging or should I say lack of paths. This was my first proper taste of country lane walking but a big enough road to have speeding traffic on, not like the country lanes I'd walked previously with Matt.

When I say speeding traffic, I mean speeding traffic, one of those sort of routes people treat as a cut through. With tree lined edges and partly embankment type verges there was no choice at times but to walk in the road.

Now and again, you'd come across a tree that had grown out to the road and if you didn't get poked in the eye, you'd get entangled in the brambles around your feet like hidden snare traps or there were hidden pot holes you could be sure to do their best to trip you or twist your ankle had I not been wearing appropriate footwear.

So yes, this all made for good training for the road that lie ahead in a few months' time. My next challenge was a blind bend, ok when you've got a verge to walk on but not so clever without.

You always try to do your best to walk facing the traffic wherever possible but there are times on dodgy old bends where it really is much safer to cross over and then cross back afterwards.

Forever conscious of the time I kept pushing my pace and just kept marching forward. Although really tempted I didn't once look at the time on my phone, I just kept putting the pressure on, surely, I was doing well, I hadn't barely eased my pace since leaving.

There were a few occasions where I had to stop and allow traffic to pass before I could proceed forward. All I could think about every time I had to stop was how the time was passing by.

As to be expected, as the morning got on the traffic was building. Just before reaching the railway crossing there were road works with a contraflow system, traffic light controlled with workmen busy working away on one side of the carriageway. Quite unusual I must say to actually see work in progress.

Usually, you get the traffic lights and the cones but no one to be seen for miles! I guess they must have been on double time or something for working on a Sunday. There was no proper footpath, I guess they just didn't contemplate on pedestrians walking down that part of the road, then comes along a nutter like me.

As I squeezed my way precariously between the traffic cones, the moving cars and the workmen, I would have thought that at least one person would have actually acknowledged me. What the hell's going wrong with this world?

Where people can't even spare a split second of their life for a simple acknowledgment of another human being, a quick eye contact or nod of the head suffice. I didn't realise I'd walk so far, maybe I'd strayed off course somewhere, lost all track of time and I was in a different neck of the woods or county even, after all, the Newbury I've become accustomed to is such a friendly town.

Then I thought of course maybe they weren't English, understood only certain things, now don't start me on that one or maybe just dam right rude. Regardless to any race or culture people can still get on. After all isn't body language about 95% of the way we communicate or something like that.

With age comes wisdom so they say and how true this is. From a very young age, we all learn a language to communicate with, even take an exam in it at some point and then go on using it for the rest of our lives. Amazingly body language of course which is the main and most useful way we communicate; we seem to spend years and years getting to grips with it and to be quite honest some people go through life never really understanding it at all.

For most of us though I think we really do get wiser as we get older. We seem to start off in our younger years reading what we want in others but as the years pass by, we gain years of practice and years of subconscious refining to really understand what people around us want or really thinking.

When somebody is saying one thing, but the body is saying another, well I know which one I believe! All gives for a worrying future when you see so many young people communicating via text.

Of course, got to the level crossing and the lights would have to be on red, wouldn't they? Why is it that even if the gates are only down 10% of the time you still have a 90% chance of catching them!

Marched on towards home, only a few miles to go, top priority now was to find myself somewhere to sit, take the wait off my feet, rehydrate myself and chuck some more calories down my hole. There's never a seat when you want one but there was a children's play park on route ahead.

Stopped at the park, so glad of a short break, stick cast aside, load off my back and a few minutes chill out, itching to peek at the time but totally resisted. I still remember now, there were a few young kids playing in adjacent park and a kid's football match was taking place on the main field, with parents clustered along the side lines.

There I sat like some kind of billy no mates or the child snatcher from chitty chitty bang bang, watching on and waiting for the right moment to pounce. Well, not actually, I was just taking a break, but you can't help wondering what parents might have been thinking. When you have children yourself, protective instincts take over involuntary.

If it was me standing there watching my son playing football or if it was my son or daughter playing in the park you can't help but wonder 'what's that billy no mates doing sitting there with his bag', even if it's just for a split second you can't help that thought entering your head.

It's such a sad world we live in that we should have to even think this way. Personally, I try to make it one of my goals in life never to judge people too quickly, never judge a book by its cover they say but how annoyingly is it that first instincts so often turn out to be true.

Oh, and while we're on the subject and without waffling on too much, the papers play a big part in this as well. The papers are just so full of doom and gloom from front to back, muggins, murders, robberies, burglaries, stabbings, shootings, plane crashes, car crashes, wars, add in a few natural disasters and it makes you wonder why anyone dare leaves the house.

How the hell can you walk down the street without suspecting everyone around you or danger on every street corner? Ok so we can put it into perspective but personally I haven't read a newspaper for years.

Can't stand them to be totally honest, I find them dam right depressing and it almost sickens me that so many people want to read that stuff every day of their lives.

Anyway, back to the walk. Break over and pressure on for the closing few miles back home. Got to my drive and having resisted checking the time since I'd set out, clocked the time and I was over the moon.

I'd made the 4 mile/hour target with a whole 5 minutes to spare. Body fine, back fine and this time feet good as well, so the two-sock system had worked perfect, result and back in time for Dan too!

# Chapter 3
# Fund Raising

Monday 18<sup>th</sup> April, decided to write a letter to St Bart's School. Well, Monday 18<sup>th</sup> was when I actually acted on it, the seed was probably sown in my head the day before while I was walking. It was never far from my mind just how I was going to raise a decent amount of money for this charity.

So many thoughts seemed to spring into my mind while walking and writing to St Bart's was one of them. Two of my boys both attend St Bart's, and I was wondering if a letter addressed to the school could help in any way to get a bit more awareness and help raise some funds.

After all, the worst that could happen would be nothing and what have I lost other than an hour of my time drafting a letter. I knew they had a school news leaflet or '*Bartholow news's* as they call it, printed regularly or more so now sent out via the email, so a short mention in this would be most helpful.

At the very least, I may even get a donation from the head mistress herself, I can't imagine she would be short of a few bob. So, I wrote direct to the head mistress. I even threw in a few leaflets I had made up in the hope they could get passed around the staff there.

About a week later, I heard back from the school. I received a letter from the head mistress herself, Mrs**! Explaining how the school was unable to help these poor children as, if they supported me, they would apparently have to say yes to everyone that ask them, so not a penny.

Of course, silly me, I didn't realise that so many parents constantly wrote to her every day and that walking 335 miles in 12 days was your average challenge that people set themselves these days. Amazingly, she even sent the leaflets back to me, which I suppose was more useful than sending them to her office shredder.

I suppose I should have offered to pay for the postage to be fair and I must try my best not to remember this the next time the school send info out asking parents for favours and support for school funding or some thing or another.

I had also been in contact with a few local papers recently, the Newbury Weekly News and also a paper over in Slough where I had originally grown up. Both the Newbury Weekly news and the Slough Observer had printed an article for me and several other papers in the Slough area had included me as well.

I must admit I was chuffed to bits at first, some public exposure. You also get your story published online as many people nowadays turn to the internet as appose to buying a paper copy. Unfortunately, the reality of it was I didn't receive a single donation, not one penny, despite every effort.

When I approached my local newspaper, it all seemed a bit too easy, they seemed more than happy to help out. They arranged for a photographer to come round to my house, took pictures of me with my stick and my walking boots held up in the air.

I had even managed to get in touch with the charity and get them to send me one of their t-shirts first class through the post, just for the occasion. All seemed such a wasted effort all in all. Great to get the exposure but pretty much a pointless exercise when not a single penny had been raised by it.

You talk to people and some of the feedback I was getting was people often keep the information and donate nearer the time or when you're actually doing the event. Was this a glimmer of hope or were people just trying to make me feel better?

Anyway, I'm a bit tougher than that and I don't get knocked of the rails that easily. I knew I had to try and do something but what was going to be the most effective method I was unsure.

I set about having some leaflets professionally printed. Up until now I had printed several handmade versions myself but decided to have one last pop at designing a leaflet and searched out a printing company on the internet.

I had about 5000 leaflets printed for about £60 and delivered within days. Surely, this would be a boost to the fundraising. So, I now needed some way of distributing them.

Totally forgetting until a few days before, the penny dropped. Monday 2nd May was bank holiday, and, on this day, there was an annual local event taking place called Newbury Crafty Craft. For those that don't know, this is about people entering teams who have to make a homemade craft to race down the Kennet and Avon canal.

I'm led to believe there are two start points, one from Kintbury and a more serious one from Hungerford. All a bit of fun really but some people really do take it quite seriously. The event finishes in Newbury at the wharf by Vicky Park which gets taken over by a mass of stalls, rides, entertainment, burger vans, tents, etc. You know, the usual things.

Maybe this could kick start this fundraising? Exposure is one thing but getting the right exposure is what counts. You really need to connect with people, be real to them and gain their trust.

I think there are so many charities and collections going on nowadays, you can be just another number plus there are so many bogus, unscrupulous wrong doers out there taking advantage of people's misfortunes, it's no wonder that Jo public can be hesitant to react. Plus, on talking to people, it would seem that not everybody felt happy donating through the internet but would be much happier donating cash.

There are a lot of people out there afraid of using the internet for the fear of identity fraud, card theft, bank details being stolen, etc. particularly the older generations. Then of course there's the other side of it, well I'll go on the internet and donate later, well surprisingly I found about one in ten actually do.

Whether they do generally forget or whether they had no intentions of doing so I'll draw my own conclusions. So anyway, I just felt like I had to get out there and connect with people, the right people!

A few days before bank holiday Monday, Friday evening in fact, I decided to enquire about having a stall at the Crafty Craft. With little expectation for leaving, it so late I sourced a contact number from the internet and called somebody.

I managed to contact one of the organisers explaining briefly what I was doing, and he very willingly managed to fit me in. This was great news but being so last minute I wasn't really that well prepared for it other than the leaflets I had had printed.

Next day, Saturday, finished work early, arrived home to an empty house. Usually I would unload my gear, jump in the bath and then call her in doors to see what the rest of the family was up to but instead today I took the opportunity to be creative.

So I popped into the garage, found a few old panels and bits of ply and knocked together a table for Monday's event. To be quite honest there's not much else in the garage despite what you're probably thinking right now. I'm not your typical hoarder at all.

In actual fact, I hate clutter. I even removed the wall units from my garage as I think the more cupboards you have the more junk you keep. If I was to class myself into one bracket or another I'd certainly be more of a minimalist.

I hate feeling closed in, I love space and the feeling of freedom. I really am an outdoor person at heart, and I must admit this was one of the things I was really looking forward to on this walk.

You hear about people having lazy days, getting up in the morning, staying in their PJ's all day, not going out the front door, watching TV all day, then going back to bed. I don't think I've ever done that in my entire life.

Realistically, I could probably count on one hand the days in my life I haven't been out anywhere, even if it's just up to the local shops or garage, it just doesn't happen, unless of course I've been ill but to be honest even that's a rarity.

Oh, here we go again, drifting off the subject. So, I pulled out a few panels from the garage, knocked together a table and a free-standing display board to sit above and even found a tin of blue paint in the garage, which was great to match in with the *Make a Wish* corporate colour scheme.

I can be a dab hand at doing things like this and if it doesn't have to be made to perfection, I can work at lightning speed. All you need is a bit of imagination and a few basic tools. We've still got two chairs that I made when the boys were little, knocked them together one afternoon in the garage on the spur of the moment.

Can't believe they've survived so well over the years considering at the time I didn't even have any sash cramps to put them together with. I guess I'll have to get rid of them one day, but I'll have to find a good home for them or maybe pass them on to the grandchildren that may would be nice.

After completing the table, I turned to the internet and downloaded some information about what the charity does, then shot up to office world in the car and purchased a laminator. Another handy little gadget for the office.

With this new information I had, along with my map of my journey, my mileage chart and my leaflets I now felt more prepared to face Joe public on Monday.

Monday morning arrived, not a bad day to start but the forecast was far from perfect. Arrived at Vicky Park at the time requested, can't remember exactly what time now but I do remember that when I got there, the majority of stalls were already set up. The boys went down with us in the car, I was to meet a chap there that would be expecting me, didn't have a clue what he looked like but just a name.

Parked up and walked round the park aimlessly, playing detective trying to track down this chap. I was to give this guy £20, my fee for having the plot. With joining the event so late no official paperwork was logged, or any details exchanged whatsoever come to that. I couldn't really have been giving this chap his lunch money, could I?

Who knows, not for me to worry about, all I was concerned with was trying to make a success of the day and raise as much money as I could for this charity. We tracked him down, paid up and he showed us to our plot. After passing a few decent plots along the way, he finally allocated a plot to us right at the end of a string of stalls.

I couldn't believe where we ended up. Right smack bang next to somebody I knew! A charity called Corner stone. I'd only recently had dealings with them, in fact I'd only just a couple of weeks ago or less fitted a kitchen in one of their properties for them.

Well that sums Newbury up all over. You can't go out in Newbury without bumping into someone you know. It can feel like quite a small town sometimes.

Anyway, nothing wrong with my location, it just meant no pressure but suddenly you feel like you're being judged. This was my first time dealing with the public in this way, I mean I've been dealing with the public for years at work but now there I was asking for the sheer generosity of people for no benefit in return.

As it goes, I didn't have a bad day. I probably did better than I expected considering the weather and low expectation I had set myself, despite the fact I am an optimist you still have to be realistic about things sometimes.

If you were always over optimistic, then you would have to deal with the fact of being let down too often which could in turn cloud your views of optimism and push you towards being a pessimist and I would never want to become like that.

Sounds a bit confusing but I know what I mean. I can't remember the exact amount I raised that day now; I could look it up as I'm sure I posted it on my web page, but it was a good first step on the ladder.

As daft as it sounds, I had this theory in my head that the more you raise the easier it is to raise or to put it the other way if you haven't raised much then other people are less likely to want to help you raise money. So, getting that initial step up the ladder is one of the hardest steps.

Human nature is a funny thing sometimes and so interesting to study. I wish I would have studied phycology when I was younger, I know it's never too late but I'm just always so busy.

There are so many things I would love to do in life but when you take away the hours of your chores of work, sleeping, eating, bathing, etc. there just never seems enough time spare. People often don't realise the hours of commitment to your job when you're self-employed.

Getting back to Vicky Park, the weather hadn't been that great. The wind had been creating havoc with my leaflets and info' documents and even took my whole board over at one point. I'd brought a few stone blocks from the garden down with me but had to request my wife to bring a few more down during the day.

I think I must have had the most exposed location in the whole of Vicky Park that day. I did eventually get rained off. Not only was I struggling with the weather, but I couldn't see the point in staying there much longer as the weather seemed to have taken its toll on the crowds, so we packed up, collapsed the table, loaded up and drove home.

Feeling slightly cheated by the short day, I decided to make one last go of it to push things a little bit further. Armed with just a pile of leaflets, I returned to Vicky Park with one of the boys in the aim of just browsing round and handing them out, after all I'd paid for the whole day.

As it turned out, it seemed like one of the best moves I could have made. Wondering around from stall to stall I got chatting to people and at one particular stall I was pointed in the direction of one particular person.

*"See that chap over there,"* someone said to me *"That's Gary Poulson, he'll have you on his radio show if you tell him what you're doing."*

All sounded great if this was true, too good an opportunity to miss, so I went straight over to him and introduced myself. Sure, enough within a few minutes of conversation I'd been invited onto his show to talk about my charity walk.

I was to be his sole guest for an hour on his live chat show on Kennet Radio in a few weeks' time. Only a local station but any publicity could surely just help and even just the thought of it sounded quite exciting. I was so glad I went back down to the park that day!

Realising how successful I had been or should I say relatively successful in comparison to the rather slow trickle of donations I had had so far, my thoughts now turned to setting up a stall in the town centre. Bit of a long shot, knowing I'd have to get permission from somebody but I was thinking of the coming Saturday.

It was now already Tuesday so it didn't leave me much time to play with. Had a few days off work which I didn't want to waste so I got straight onto the internet and found some contact details for the council. I was hoping to set up stall in the market square outside the old town hall.

So, I called Newbury council only to be told I had to get permission from Newbury Bid as they controlled the streets. So, I then got in touch with Newbury Bid only to be told that I couldn't set up at this location on Saturday as the market controlled that area that day and that I needed to get in touch with the market and ask permission from them.

All in all, what I thought would be just a few calls turned out to be quite a challenge and again another commitment of more time and energy. I also had to fill out a form from Newbury council to apply for a street trading license, which I had to wait for to be processed.

I had to fill out forms for the market to get permission for the plot, plus on top of this I had to purchase public liability insurance in case some dozy person happen to trip on the leg of my table or something like that.

When I first started ringing around for public liability, I must admit I had a bit of a shock. Yet again more money I was having to plough in from my own pocket, I must admit I came close to forgetting the whole idea of having the stall until one of the lovely members of staff managed to recommend me to an insurance company that specialised in market traders.

What a relief to find this company, they were in a different price bracket. I took a brief look through the small print, always caution of course as to why they were so much cheaper but couldn't find anything obvious.

No doubt somewhere hidden in the small print were the words that spelt out that in the event of a serious accident or if somebody had a serious leg injury, they were not covered for a proper prosthetic limb or a wooden leg of some kind but merely a chipboard pole that would disintegrate the first time they went out in the rain! Anyway, what I did know was this was the only policy I could afford.

Although the market was very kindly setting up a gazebo for me, I had to go out and purchase a fold up table from somewhere. Using the chipboard/plywood makeshift table, I had knocked up was out of the question, I needed something lightweight so I could park up somewhere close to the town and walk in with everything I needed either hanging from my two arms or loaded on to my back in a rucksack.

Saturday seemed to fly round. I was up early, washed, dressed and breakfast done, loaded up and set off to meet somebody at the market square for 7:30 am if I recall correctly.

Parked as close to the town as I could, free of charge, mind that's a rare thing to be able to do these days. Marched round to the market place like an overworked donkey. I think my arms must have been a good three inches longer by to time I came to rest.

I was loaded down with table, chair, stick, table cover, notice board, cash box leaflets, water, food, paperwork and even a pile of bricks to stop the wind from causing havoc! Weren't sure exactly where I was to be positioned but as luck had it ended up right outside the old town hall, just where I wanted to be.

Didn't take me long to set up but to be quite honest 7:30am on a Saturday morning was a wee bit early to catch any appropriate passers-by so I just tried to relax, chilled out and enjoyed the fresh morning air.

Sat and watched the other market traders setting up their stalls. The work that some of these people put into setting up and then packing away at the end of the day is just incredible. God knows what time some of these get up in the morning!

Wasn't that relaxing sitting there half the time, I had a huge lorry almost within touching distance as they offloaded their goods to a stall nearby. Any trivial number of passers-by that were around that time in the morning were barely going to see me hiding behind a big lump of metal on wheels.

Then of course you have to remember that the vast majority of these people would actually be rushing around on a mission to get to work, be it in the town centre or to the train station.

I remember the market coordinator chap coming over and suggesting I was in the wrong place and should really be up in the high street somewhere, he'd been watching me apparently and seen the lack of interest so far.

I wasn't fussed to be honest as I really wasn't expecting anything to happen until at least 9 o'clock. Besides, Newbury Bid had already told me that the high street plot had already been allocated for that day.

Didn't have a bad day all in all. What was really fantastic was the fact that during the day I'd actually met several people that knew of someone quite close to them that had actually benefited from the charity.

The feedback I received from them was absolutely fantastic and was a credit to the charity as well as giving me a mental boost to keep on course, plus it also made it feel so much more real. Of course, not everybody shared the same view, as I have already said people are all so different.

It was a case of very quickly becoming quite thick-skinned or you could very easily become totally demoralised, wonder whether you should be there campaigning at all and pack up and go back home. Fortunately, you soon learned to stick it out knowing that for every negative vibe you received from someone there was always a greater positive one just around the corner.

Some people couldn't praise you enough for what you were trying to do while others would try to make you feel like some kind of second-class citizen begging or touting for business to get people to sign up for some kind of charity scam or something similar.

The hand up in front was a good one with the shaking head or they'd briefly listen to what you had to say or not rather and simply say:

*"No thanks!"*

That sometimes felt a bit harsh, I always thought that the British people were supposed to be a polite nation so was expecting more of a:

*"Sorry, I'm in a rush!"* or *"sorry, I've got no cash!"* or *"I'll have a look on your website later,"* and take a leaflet with them. Well at least I suppose you knew where you stood.

Then of course there were times when you bumped into people you knew or complete strangers that wanted to chat and chat. This was of course a bit of a dilemma for as much as you wanted to chat, in the back of your mind the clock was ticking and you could be missing vital customers as they strolled on by.

There were only so many times I was going to get the opportunity to set up stall in the town before the event and so far, it seemed to be proving to be the best form of fund raising or should I say almost the only way.

The end of the day was drawing near, the market traders had nearly all packed up and gone home. My gazebo had been removed and collapsed and I was debating about packing up myself.

Annie and Dan had come down to meet us during the afternoon and hadn't really taken much during the last hour, once again we'd been surrounded by trucks reloading their unsold market stock.

I was just thinking should we pack up now or hang on for that last donation, then out of the blue came a really freak strong gust of wind, taking my board over, my laminates off the table and my leaflets spread across the market square pavement like huge confetti lumps at a wedding.

My decision was now final, it seemed like a sign, so after gathering stock we packed up for the day and got my gear back to the car. I now had two successful days behind me and with a great boost to the fund raising, I now felt compelled to keep going.

Once again, my family had put up with me spending one of my only few days off work totally consumed by this charity walk event but they seemed so supportive which was quite a relief.

I had totally underestimated the time and commitment involved when I came up with this whole crazy idea but was now far too committed to stop. Besides, the more I raised and the closer the date drew near, the more real it all felt and the more determined I felt to see it right through!

Matt was down in Dartmoor for the weekend with the school, taking part in his Ten Tours challenge. He was due to reach the finish line sometime on Sunday and we had been invited to go and see him in.

Despite having to miss out on a potential football match for Dan, we decided to travel down and give our support. I say a potential match for as it goes in the end it was cancelled, so he didn't miss out on much.

We arrived down in Dartmoor early Sunday afternoon, there were hundreds if not thousands of parents there. The whole event was organised by the MOD and seemed very well organised despite the fact that we had no idea where Matt was finishing or even if he was actually still walking.

There were burger vans doted around everywhere and the odd trade stall and I couldn't help but wonder just how much I could have raised there. See the difference there would have been that people could relate to what I was doing.

One thing I had noticed at Vicky Park and at the high street stalls was a pattern forming. Not 100% proof but I had noticed that with the older generation it tended to be the ladies that were donating, I think it was that mother child bond that was the driving pin and with the younger generations it tended to be 50/50 as they could relate to their own children.

Surprisingly in between it tended to be the men that would donate as I think they could more easily and realistically relate to the physical challenge that lay ahead. Some men would take a real interest in the route I was planning, the miles I was covering, the hours I would be walking, luggage, footwear, etc.

Then there were some of the funniest comments I would get from some people that were only half listening to what I was saying and when I explained I'd be walking 335miles in12 days, I'd get:

*"No thanks, I couldn't do that!"* I could only laugh and say:

*"No, not you, me!"*

Anyway, so getting back to Dartmoor, I was thinking, all these crowds of people here and nearly all would be able to relate to the challenge I had set. Mind even if I had been able to arrange a stall there it wouldn't have been practical.

It was so exposed there and with the wind cutting across lie a knife I'd have been lucky to have kept my plastic fold up table on the ground, let alone any paperwork on it. I'd have been in Dartmoor and my table would have ended up back in Exeter.

We were on time to see Matt cross the finish line, he'd done about 55miles in 2 days and slept in a tent! He looked a bit grubby, sunburnt and knackered but he'd had a great experience.

We hung around for him and his mates to collect their medals and have their photos done while up on the podium like all the other competitors there, then set off on our long trip back home. Another long day had come to a close. Matt's walk was now over but mine was still to come.

# Chapter 4
# Media

Monday 9th May, spent some time gathering thoughts from the weekend. Just how was I going to raise the bar and try to reach my target? How was I going to keep the money coming in? I needed more exposure, so I set about writing a very short letter that I could send to various newspapers, just a few short sentences to capture some interest in what I was trying to do.

The chances were that I would be up against it trying to get people interested enough to print something but what had I to lose. I systematically searched on the internet for newspapers all the way down from London to Land's End with the idea that I would contact them explaining that I would be stopping in their area or passing through, obviously appealing for the public to donate, bear in mind this is a national charity.

So, I collated a list of newspapers, as many as I could in the hope that if only one or two get back to us, this would be a success. What did I have to lose other than my own time? As I've already said I put a lot more hours into this than I had ever considered necessary. If I remember rightly, it ended up quite late to bed that night.

Up early Tuesday morning and got straight on with it sending this initial letter out to every newspaper editor you can imagine. I then had a much more detailed letter I had constructed for anybody interested along with some photos of myself kitted out for walking.

Well surprise, surprise, most of the emails might just have well been mailed to the office shredder or the office bin. I did however hear back from a few. The common theme seemed to be 'do you live in this area?'

Of course, if I didn't, they were not interested! I must admit I did find this a little strange and made my thoughts quite clear to those editors by saying:

"I may not live in your area but this charity does!"

After all this is a national charity and children all over the country are helped regardless to where the money has come from!

I did have one success, though of course falling into the above criteria, as an editor of a Basingstoke newspaper was keen to speak to me. He called me, we had a brief interview or chat or whatever you want to call it by phone and he seemed keen to get something printed ASAP. Adam Flin if I remember rightly.

They run a Newbury and Thatcham edition newspaper and he was keen to get a story published in the very next edition that week. Due out on Thursday I must admit I had my reservations that they would get a story turned round that quickly, mind he did sound quite convincing on the phone.

Wednesday was another eventful day. I planned to set up a stall in the town centre to do a bit more fund raising. This time I'd requested a high street location, just in front of St Nick's Church.

Had to go through all the usual old rigmarole again with the council and Newbury Bid and of course get my insurance in place again for the day. Didn't really turn out to be a very good day in the end.

The weather was against us which was really frustrating as I'd originally planned to do this on the Thursday but due to following the weather predictions, Thursday wasn't looking that great and Wednesday was forecast as the better day of the two.

How wrong they were. Wednesday turned out to be a crap day. Of course, you couldn't just turn up with your stall when you feel like it as you have to get all the correct permission and paper work in place first.

Didn't set up stall until about 10am as until 10am the high street is open to free-flowing traffic and being during the week it can get quite busy at times, so late start anyway. Parked in a carpark if I remember, Strawberry Hill, £5 for the day. Didn't get off to a bad start but all really went downhill from then.

Mid to late morning, merrily minding my own business on my stall, when I was blessed with the company of how should I put it, one of Newbury's less desirables. With the churchyard directly behind me there was always going to be a need to keep an eye on things, not that you really have too much to worry about in Newbury.

What I wasn't prepared for mind was what happened next. So along comes this lady who decided to park herself down on the public bench next to me. Not an awful lot I could do about that to be honest but harmless enough as she was, she really did put a dampener on things.

After trying to make light conversation with me, she then reached into her rucksack pulled out a drink and made herself quite at home on the bench. What's wrong with that you're thinking, well how about adding to that she also had her own stereo type music system on her back, pumping out her own crazy music.

You could see she had made herself almost too comfortable and for as long as she was there, the entire space around me had become like some kind of a no-fly zone for pedestrians. I felt like I was being held hostage at my own stall and there was nothing I could do about it.

I felt like I daren't speak to her as this would only encourage her to stay longer and I remember feeling so peeved off knowing how much effort had gone into being there, the clock was ticking and my time really was being wasted.

I was beginning to think she was going to be there all day and was half tempted to pack up, call it a day and go home. I couldn't tell you how relieved I was when she finally got up and marched off.

Surely nothing else was going to go wrong today now? Well, it did. As I said, the weather forecast had completely changed from when I booked this slot and I was now expecting a possible shower around about lunch time. I had prepared myself with a big umbrella and a spare top just in case I got a good soaking.

What I wasn't prepared for however was how heavy and prolonged this shower was, virtually torrential rain. I sat there under this umbrella for almost an hour and a half. I must have looked like a right fool sitting it out but I really hadn't had a good day so far and I was determined to make something of it, trouble was the clouds seemed almost static.

It was as if that lady had put some kind of curse on me. The clouds were building for some time from all around, gradually getting darker and darker but when the heavens opened, the clouds seemed to come to a complete stop. I could see a beautiful blue sky on the horizon but it just never seemed to get any closer.

There was a very kind lady from a charity shop opposite, Helen & Douglas I think, she braved the rain and came over to me with a dry top pulled from one of the racks in her shop, so kind of her. I put it on the back of my chair. I had brought one of my own but I seemed to be escaping the worst of the downpour as long as I kept huddled up tight into my chair and had the umbrella positioned ok.

Unfortunately, the rain was so bad that the stall took a bit of a knock too. The blue paint was starting to run away from the notice board and water was even finding its way into the laminated posters and info' sheets I had.

Worst of all was the manual donation sheets, I really thought they were safe and free from harm but silly me as the rain cleared and I lifted the front cover of the file they were in I had a bit of a shock. Straight into panic mood!

Water had poured straight into the binder and instead of having several sheets of donations I now had just one thick sheet with blue and black ink running a mock all over. What would happen to all the donations I'd raised so far; ok I had the money but people had gift aided and without these details all would be lost.

I got straight on the phone to my wife, she came straight down to town, paid Smiths a visit on the way past, bought me some dry stationary, retrieved the wet ones from me, took them back home and began the delicate task of separating the sheets and drying them all back out.

Annoyingly I then had to spend the rest of the afternoon putting people details down on a blank piece of paper rather than a proper purpose made letter headed one, which didn't exactly look that professional but still at least I got a few more donations, all three of them!

I did pack up early in the end, I'd had a crap day all in all. The sheets dried out fully and all the writing was readable and my wife washed the top from the charity shop and took it back into her the next day.

Did at least have some success with the donations, not what I was hoping for but every penny counts. Maybe I was setting myself unrealistic goals in my head. There's a fine balance in promoting something you believe in and not being a nuisance to those that aren't interested, especially when it comes to extracting money from the public.

One of the problems I found was that many people naturally assumed that you were trying to get them to sign up to some kind of contract, then also because of the location I was at, some thought I was something to do with church. The politer ones would take a leaflet and say that they'd go on line and donate later and there was a small number of these that actually did!

One great success was a gentleman that actually went off to his cash machine and came back with some cash to donate, then there was a lady that had just got her pension and wanted to donate.

Not that I'd had the best of days today but I did also meet some more people that had benefitted directly from the charity and couldn't praise the charity enough. This was always great to hear, all made it seem so much more worthwhile.

It's amazing when you spend a while in Newbury town centre how many faces you recognise from day to day, you find yourself talking to people that have previously donated without at first realising, then the penny would drop.

Thursday morning, my wife and I just happened to be in Basingstoke, can't remember exactly why now, there may not even have been a reason, we often pop to different towns if I manage to get a day off work, as long as were back home for when the boys get home from school.

It's not uncommon for us to even pop down to the coast for a few hours like Portsmouth for instance. A nice casual stroll along the seafront, browse around the shops in peace without those glum teenage faces that didn't really want to be there but always would be, then grab a spot of lunch somewhere before returning home.

Anyway, so we picked up a copy of the local paper on the off chance there would be a story somewhere inside but no, nothing. Well hopefully it would be in next weeks.

On our way back, my wife remembered something we'd forgotten to pick up. It may have been something for one of the boys for school, something for their cooking, I can't remember now but anyway, we decided to shoot into Newbury town centre on the way back. Shot in to the multi-storey, then shot round Tesco's, had to be quick as we were running tight for time.

Front of the store, just inside the window, great big stack of papers, hot off the press and there I was! Front page headlines, huge letters splashed across the front page, 'MAMMOTH WALK FOR CHARITY!' picture included and continued on the next page.

Couldn't believe it, Adam Flinn had really come up trumps for me. Couldn't really ask for better publicity than that. I was chuffed to bits with his report, surely this would help raise some funds.

Friday flew round and I was due on air on Kennet Radio at five o'clock. I wondered down to the town and arrived outside the radio station with a good ten minutes to spare. I always usually arrive places on time or slightly early, it's just something I've always done, mind if you're going on to a live broadcast being late isn't really an option.

Arrived at the correct location but weren't too sure where to go when I got there, ended up giving Gary a buzz. He was just on his way so I waited back out at the front for him. He was cutting it fine I'd say but I guess when you do that sort of thing all the time, you become quite relaxed about the whole thing.

In the same way, I would be relaxed going into someone's house to look at their kitchen because I've done it for so many years. I suppose you could say he was just being efficient; I like efficiency that happens to be right up my street.

So, we went up into the studio where he introduced me to the sound engineer and they both made me feel very relaxed. I'd actually been quite looking forward to doing this as I'd never done anything like this before. I'd say I'm quite a confident person anyway.

This has been built through life's paths, sometimes chosen, sometimes not and years of self-analysation. Yes, if you went back thirty something years ago, back to my school days, I was a completely different person then.

Never had much confidence in myself as a child but at the same time still had a strong personality underneath, strong enough to never want to follow anyone or be easily led, happy to do things my way. Just never had the confidence to stand out but as I've grown this never seems to bother me.

I certainly don't go out of my way to stand out like some individuals do but at the same time I am very strong willed and very individual. Put in a room with a hundred people, if ninety-nine wanted to go one way and I wanted to go the other I would happily go the other way, that's just me, I don't think I'll ever change.

Little story, few years back and it was a few years now I can tell Ya, crazy things you do in your younger days, I remember going up to Scotland with a group of lads to pick up a friend, five of us in the car going up, six of us in the car coming back.

Straight from the pub on a Saturday night, car was clapped out, totally clapped out, can't remember now what was wrong with it but do remember push starting it to get it going again every time we had to stop. On the way back we had to pull off the motorway near the Lake District with engine troubles, didn't get far down this dual carriageway before the engine virtually blow up!

Oil, nuts, bolts, the lot, all over the road. After catching a lift from a local highway patrol so as to use a phone, Sconny the driver made contact with his friends back in Scotland and arranged for a pick-up truck to come all the way down from Stranraer. And yes, you did hear me correctly, we got a lift to a phone box, unheard of nowadays in this mobile world.

Anyway, so this truck was now on its way down to us and was due to reach us about one o'clock in the morning. We all had a chat about which way we were going to go when the truck turned up and as it turned out all five of them come to the conclusion it was better to go back to Scotland instead of going in the direction we were heading, bear in mind we were approximately half way between the two. I had already made up my mind I was heading home.

So, there I was in the middle of January, must have been about -5C outside, that was without the wind chill factor, thin cotton shirt on my back and a ten mile walk to Kendal or a choice or returning to Scotland in the wrong direction. Sunday evening it was, I had work the next day and I decided I was going to be there even if it meant arriving late.

So, this truck turns up and I think all five lads were shocked when I got out of the car, turned my back on them and walked off into the darkness on my own. It was absolutely pitch black, could barely see where I was walking and every time a car came along, their headlights were really blinding as your eyes tried to adjust to the light as they passed you by.

Eventually another police patrol vehicle came by, stopped, picked me up and gave me a lift to Kendal train station. I don't remember how many hours I spent there but I do remember the bitter coldness as I spent the rest of the night in a telephone box in front of the station gates, just trying to stay warm.

You may not remember now but they use to have a small ledge that poked out that housed the phone books. I tried to perch myself up on this ledge as the walls of the telephone box didn't actually reach all the way down to the floor and the cold air that was blowing across my feet felt quite perishing as the ground outside glistened with frost. With not even a watch to my name the night seemed endless.

When the station eventually opened the next day, I huddled myself against a heater in the waiting room but could barely contain my shivering as the cold night air seemed to have got right down into my bones. I'm pretty sure I had a mild case of hypothermia or worse.

When I got back Monday morning, I never did actually make it to work, as it goes, I spent the whole week off suffering badly from tonsillitis and some self-inflicted flu type thing. It was rare for me to be ill like this but I guess I'd just pushed my body too far and the germs had just taken over.

Mind I was always quite susceptible to tonsillitis when I was younger. Still don't regret my decision, despite the fact if I would have gone back to Scotland that night, I would have actually got back to work sooner as I'm sure I wouldn't have been ill.

Getting back to the studio. Time was fast approaching five and we took our seats. There I was, about to go live on air, a big mic in front of my face, headphones on and awaiting Gary's countdown from the engineer. I do remember him saying to me.

*"Just relax and imagine we're down the pub having a chat,"* and it sort of just drifted along from there.

I was surprised how quickly the hour passed. He'd play a tract then introduce me with some light chat then play another track. In between tracks he'd half allow me to prepare for what was coming next, so there were no big shocks. He played music of my own choice which I must admit did help me to relax.

At the end of each track would be a count down before going back on air. My boys were tuned in at home, listening live and one of my neighbours may well have been listening too as I bumped into her on my way down to the studio.

The interview went really well. Ok so there may not have been thousands of listeners and out of them only a small percentage interested enough to even think about donating but it was a great experience and every little bit of promotion would help.

All a bit of fun as well, I had to take part in Gary Poulson's biscuit challenge. I had to dunk a biscuit in to a hot cup of tea, hold it in there and remove it on Gary's count. The clock was ticking as it had to be held horizontally and the challenge was to see how long it took before the biscuit collapsed.

You needed a good steady hand, oh and an engineer that didn't jog the table, mind I did get a five second bonus award for that and still didn't make it up on to the leader board, didn't even come close!

I'd also taken some newspapers down with me to the studio and in particular, the local observer where I had front page coverage. Gary made a good point of this during his broadcast but looking back now, it was a real struggle getting any kind of what I would call effective advertising.

I think there are just so many charities around now and so many people doing special things to raise money for so many well deserving causes that it really is hard to get people to tune in to yours and get them to react.

At the end of the show, Gary sent a link to my computer and I was able to listen to whole interview again at home. That's a bit weird listening to yourself but I was more than happy with it and posted it on my Facebook page.

I've never been one for giving up easily and over the next week I racked my brains for different ways of getting media coverage. I sent further emails to a few local radio stations and even sent one to an official contact point for Lenny Henry himself as he has connections with Premier Inn Hotels.

Wednesday evening 18th May, I had a brain wave. I drafted up a letter to my local MP Richard Benyon. My thinking behind this was if I could get the support of Richard Benyon behind me, this would not only give us a chance of getting back into the papers and maybe even front page but might also help carry some weight.

So, I drafted up a letter and the following day my wife dropped it off at his office by hand. It was in the back of my mind that day that I may just get a call from him or his secretary but to be quite honest I didn't really expect anything.

Anyway, there I was working away that Thursday afternoon when my phone started buzzing and sure enough it was Richard Benyon's secretary. My wife had only dropped the letter off a short while ago and I'd received an almost instant reaction.

*"Richard would love to have his photo done with you,"* she said.

Yet again, I was chuffed to bits with my new accomplishment and got straight on the phone to Newbury Weekly News and Newbury Observer to see if they could arrange a photographer out to meet us there. I'd arranged to meet up with Richard the very next day, Friday afternoon so no time to waste.

All was going well and sounded too good to be true. Finished work early on Friday, I was working all the way over in Slough so I didn't want to get caught up in any traffic getting back over to Newbury. Not usually quite so far away but it does happen from time to time, when I get recommended by friends or family or maybe a friend of a previous client or somebody may have moved or relocated etc.

So anyway, I made it back to Richard's office on time and so did one of the photographers. Unfortunately, the reporter from Newbury Observer didn't, I received a call about half an hour prior to arriving explaining that he'd somehow locked his keys in his car or locked himself out of the office or something like that, which was a shame as I think this was my best hope of getting back onto the front page.

Had a short interview with Richard, he didn't have a lot of spare time to spend with us but I was glad of him squeezing me in to be honest, particularly at such short notice as he was due to go away very shortly.

Newbury Weekly News photographer took loads of snaps inside and outside the office with Richard and a few of Richard and me with plans laid out on the table, discussing the route I was taking. Didn't manage to get any snaps myself but did get a few that Richard's secretary took of us and kindly emailed to me.

He also posted me on some social media page as well, not sure which one now, not that it turned out to be of any real gain. Yet again always seemed so strange that so many people that would tell you what a fantastic thing you were doing seemed so keen to help and so willing to pass your details on to others yet not actually make any kind of donation themselves. Quite frustrating at times, I can tell you.

Did manage to get my story printed again in both papers, along with a picture of myself with Richard but all yet again to no avail. It would seem that the only way to get people to donate was to personally meet them, people that wanted to personally help and not just pass your name on to other.

It just seemed so strange that so many that told you how fantastic it was what you were doing would do anything but put their hand in their own pocket!

# Chapter 5
# Final Preps

With the clock still ticking and my walk getting closer and closer, my thoughts were now turning to training or lack of it, should I say. Up until this point, I'd never actually done a 30-mile walk. I mean, I still didn't know what it was like to do a 30-mile walk, let alone get up the next day and do it all over again, plus of course some days I'd be walking even further than that!

So, I planned a route from my house, a circular route with no public transport involved so I could set off and finish whatever time I liked. The initial mapped out route didn't quite add up to the full 30 miles so I had to play around with it, stretch it out here and there with a few detours. The other big difference was this time, I decided to carry a lot more weight to try to make it as realistic as possible.

So, Sunday 22nd May, I set off on the big one. Glad I done the detours first as I may not have ended up doing the extra distance had it have been at the end of the walk. I did toy around in my mind which way round to do the walk and as it was, I was definitely right to do it the way I did as it wasn't the easiest walk I've done.

Set off at one hell of a pace determined to keep to the 4 mile/hour pace even with my load so I pushed myself fairly hard. Set myself a goal of not stopping until I'd reached the village of Aldermaston, which would be about half way so about 15 miles. So, I reached Aldermaston, recharged the batteries, rehydrated myself and set off again after allowing myself just a short rest.

Legs were feeling more tired this time and my feet were aching a little. Worst of all was a cramping feeling in one of my legs. Was this because I'd sat down and allowed my muscles to cool down too much or simply pushing myself too far or maybe lacking in fluids. Whichever it was I knew I had no choice but to push on walking through the pain.

Going up and out of Aldermaston, up towards AWE *(the atomic weapons establishment)* the sidewalks were fairly uneven in places, not really designed for pedestrians and the rising gradient just put more and more pressure on my legs. I remember at one point I actually fell over backwards onto the grass verge, a combination I think of tired legs, sore feet and the weight on my back pulling me off balance.

I must admit I did feel a bit of an idiot stumbling backwards but it also made me more aware of just how dangerous my task was. I could quite easily have fallen back the other way and landed in the road.

On from AWE and upwards towards Ashford Hill, heading towards the main A339 Basingstoke to Newbury Road. I had to do a fair bit of walking along the actual road itself where footpaths and verges tended to be either un-walkable or non-existent. Found myself stopping more regularly for fluid and also felt like I was slowing down with the pace.

Maybe I'd just pushed myself too far today but I was sure that either way this was all the better as a training exercise. I must admit the route was beginning to feel a bit endless and I still had a good 10 miles or more ahead of us.

I reached the A339 and proceeded back west towards Newbury. This was my first real taste of having to walk a main road actually in the road. There wasn't really any practical footpath to walk on and I also found it had become a real struggle to walk on such uneven ground when your feet are feeling very sore.

With the weight pulling on your back, it also becomes a bit risky trying not to go flying over on the rough terrain with sore feet and aching legs all adding to your instability. It did feel a little scary with trucks thundering towards you so I did my best to avoid road walking wherever possible.

As I proceeded towards Newbury that day, the thought did enter my head, do I take my phone out of my pocket and call a taxi? But I daren't do this as this as this would have been like quitting before I'd started. After all, if I couldn't handle this simple 30-mile walk, how the hell was I going to survive 12 days of it?

So, with sore feet and cramp in my legs I was having a little argument in my head but I just had to see it through. In all honesty I think I had just pushed myself far too much when considering my speed, distance, load on my back and my lack of training!

By the time I was within spitting distance of Newbury, I was having serious cramp problems in both of my legs and with my legs feeling so stiff, I was almost stomping home, putting even more pressure onto already sore feet.

I'd learnt a good lesson today but had I pushed myself too far? Had I concurred another physical issue or had I caused myself unnecessary damage which was about to hinder me when I did my real walk?

I was also having problems with my left ankle and it didn't dawn on me until that day that I'd woken up an old injury. My left ankle had become swollen on top and was painful to walk with movement becoming more and more restricted.

Thinking back this happened a few years ago when I went on a walk with the family, finishing up at Savernake Forest over in Marlborough. At the time, I sort of assume that something had got down inside my left sock and bitten me but with the exact pain in the same location, all now seemed so obvious, I'd set off an old injury from an incident years ago at work.

Years ago, I stepped back badly off the bottom step of a ladder somehow placing my toes down the wrong way. As I felt my full body weight bearing down on my toes, I was forced to throw myself backwards and went flying down to the ground, half-breaking my fall with my arms but falling back at such a speed, managing to slightly bash the back of my head on impact.

So, one minute, I'm descending from a small ladder after throwing out some trash, then the next I'm lying on my back in pain. My head was fine but the problem was my toes were still underneath my left foot.

I must have stretched my left ankle right out of its socket and for a while, I was stuck lying on the concrete unable to move. I could feel a weird sensation running up my leg from my left foot. I managed to turn over onto my side and pull myself up onto my other foot.

My left foot was swollen for several days and I was unable to work or even drive my car. I never went to see anyone about it and at the time didn't really consider that I'd done any permanent damage. That's the problem when you injure yourself, things are never quite the same again.

A bit like one of my big toes only bends so far round from when I kicked something once. So, I now had this injury back to haunt me. I just hoped I hadn't aggravated it too much as I had one hell of a walk still ahead of us!

Reached top end of town and collapsed down for a rest. Called the boys to come up and meet me, a bit of moral support and relief from the rucksack I was carrying. My legs really did feel like they'd taken a pounding and were in a lot more pain than I was expecting them to be.

Hopefully just like all the other previous annoyances, all would be ok on my next walk, I was just so pleased I'd managed to do the training I had, little as it may be but turned out to be an essential part of physical training to help prepare me for the real thing.

By the time the boys had met up with me, I'd reached the high street. We sat for a while then proceeded home handing out leaflets down the high street as we passed through. From my experience so far, the chance of someone donating off the back of a leaflet was slim but what had we to lose and we were slowly but surely running out of time for fund raising.

The boys had recently started to post leaflets door to door locally in the hope that somebody just might want to donate. Well from the hundreds of leaflets that were dispatched door to door there were literally only a few people that donated and I'm so thankful to them.

We made one last ditch attempt of fund raising on the high street before I walked. On Saturday 5th June, I set up stall back outside the church. As optimistic as ever I was banking on having a good day but it just wasn't to be. The weather was great, couldn't have been better for standing there but unfortunately a little too nice.

As I'd already discovered on previous occasions there seemed to be a trend to the people that donated. These people were nowhere to be seen. The town was sort of busy but with people with only one thing on their agenda, themselves.

Yes, that day the town was busy with under dressed men and women with their chests pushed out and heads held high, all desperate for a ray of sunshine and a chance of catching someone's eye to boost their own ego!

Donating to a cause other than their own would have been like prising a bone from a dog. I mean there were some other folks around but the odds were really stacked against us I'm afraid. The afternoon was a little better as it had clouded over a bit and the older generation had decided to come out of hibernation.

Packed up early in the end, I think I'd just about had enough and reached the conclusion that my hanging around was more in vain than of any real sub sequential benefit. To be quite honest I felt I'd put enough effort in now and was pretty much at the point at whatever had now been achieved, was pretty much my limit, with the time now against me and my walk now imminent.

Unless you're famous or dealing with people with some direct link to the cause, I found fund raising to be an extremely difficult task and I now take my hat off to people that do it. I think if I had been trying to raise money for cancer research for instance, which everybody can relate to or maybe feel they may benefit themselves one day, I think fund raising may have been a slight bit easier but I'm glad to of chosen the charity I did and would be happy to support them again in the future should the opportunity arise.

Realising how difficult it can be, I have a completely different view now when I come across genuine individuals trying to raise money for good causes, they believe in. I'm so much more likely to donate now than I was before.

Anyway, despite not achieving my goal I had originally set out to do, I was proud of my achievement so far and as my walk was drawing ever closer my thoughts were now on final preparations for the journey. All well and good raising this money but now I had to prove myself mentally and physically and I'd promised myself not to fail.

Can't remember if I've mentioned it or not but my mate decided to come on board after all. He wasn't going to do the full walk with me but was due to join us about half way along at Honiton. This was great news!

Mentally, I was now ready to tackle whatever was about to be thrown at me and that was just as well as you'll soon discover. Physically though not so great! My left ankle had now been playing up ever since one of my many, many training walks *(all four of them!)* and knowing that it was unlikely to heal anytime soon, I paid the doctors a visit for some advice and some anti-inflammatories.

Of course, what it really needed was rest but with 335 miles ahead of us and a heavy load, that was looking pretty unlikely. To top this off, I had also had a problem recently with one of my toes on my right foot, don't ask me why but my little toe on my right foot was also giving me grief and about two weeks before I was due to set off on this walk, my small toe nail decided to come away.

For some reason, my toe was extremely sensitive and just the pressure of the inside of my boot up against it or too much sock against it and it made normal walking most uncomfortable. So, all in all not a great start!

I had a busy week at work knowing that I had to get my jobs finished as I'd be away for the next two weeks. Last thing I wanted to do was to leave a customer with a half-finished job or incomplete to any extent. I also had a bit of running around to do for the family as my wife doesn't drive, so making sure any real heavy shopping or other chores were done where possible.

Impossible to get all the shopping mind, the boys eat like horses. I'm sure there's a hole in the back of the fridge, you fill it up one day and the next morning, it's half empty again! I know Matt and Dan are both teenagers but I never remember eating constantly like they do when I was their age.

The week flew round and before I knew it, it was Saturday. Final check with all my gear to load up. I seemed to have so much stuff to cram into my rucksack. I may have been going over the top I don't know but I had a spare pair of shoes to take. I had this horrible vision in my head of what if my boots decided to fall apart?

With so many miles to cover in such a short space of time it wasn't like I could divert to the nearest town centre and pick up another pair. It's not as if I could jump in the car and go down the road and back.

It happened to me once before on a family walk a few years ago, trekking the outskirts of Marlborough, in the middle of nowhere, miles from the car and my sole decided to come completely away from one of my boots, flopping right back to the heel.

The only way I could continue to walk along was to lift my knee so high and take almost leaps forward to allow for my flapping sole else I was likely to rip the whole thing off which would of gave for a very uncomfortable walk indeed! Walking along like Coco the Clown wasn't the answer either so I kept an eye out for a solution.

First, I found some string and managed to tie my boots back together with that but not really being a great design for the bottom of your boots that quite quickly perished. I then upgraded this with some heavier grade string but my ultimate solution to get me out of trouble was a length of thick wire which I found dangling from a farmer's fence.

It was about to fall off, honest! It was a good job I had a strong grip as bending it with my bare hands took some doing, I can tell you! It may have looked a bit strange and the boys though it looked hilarious but it sure lasted the journey ok.

So, getting back to my packing. I also had a spare satnav; I ordered a cheap one-off amazon just in case my existing one didn't last the whole day. I couldn't think of anything worse than getting almost to your destination then losing the directions for the last few miles or running off course one day and having to walk back the way you'd come from, adding more miles to your journey. Staying on track on the right route would be really critical.

My wife had sorted out a whole bundle of first aid equipment, half of Boots the Chemist in fact! I had no choice but to go through the lot and eliminate at least half of it and keep to what I considered to be the bare essentials. I had a clean change of top for every day as washing clothes wasn't really an option.

I had a few *Make a Wish* t-shirts from the charity. Ideally, I wanted one for every day but they wanted to charge me for further tops, so instead they agreed to send me a special bib. Turned out to be a great help as the bib stood out a lot more than the t-shirt, so was better for safety plus of course, I could wear it over the top of my waterproofs should I wear them or should I say when.

Needed two pairs of socks a day but didn't really want to take 24 pairs as I was taking proper walking socks, not your thin summer ones, so I came up with a plan that allowed me to wear each pair for two days but always have a fresh pair on my feet.

By wearing the inside pair on the outside the next day, this almost halved the socks I needed. Well, my plans didn't quite work out that way as you'll find out as you read on.

Of course, there was also all the paperwork I needed to carry, my Premier Inn confirmation sheets, all laminated for protection from moisture, a few mileage charts and maps and things and as many heath snacks like protein bars, etc. that I could, to ration out through the course of my journey.

I also had a light weight pair of shoes to wear to dinner in the evening and a light weight zip up top to wear if it were a bit chilly in the mornings. All in all, there seemed to be a lot of gear to carry even after I'd gone through and just kept what I considered to be the bare essentials.

By Saturday evening my bag was packed and I felt about as mentally prepared for this as I could be. A bit anxious I guess about the lack of training I'd done but never the less eager now to just get stuck in and get on with it.

One thing I have forgotten to mention was the state of my heels. Several weeks earlier I'd made this silly decision to do something about the huge clumps of hard skin on the back of my heels. Thinking I was doing the right thing I set about removing some of it before attempting this marathon. Bad, bad, decision.

Maybe had I have done this well before now all would have been good but all I had managed to achieve was to leave the remaining skin on both my heels extremely sore. I was worrying about the hard skin splitting open and causing me sore areas during my walk but in interfering I had created huge sensitive areas on both heels just when I didn't need it! My heels both felt like massive carpet burns and I hadn't even started yet!

So physically, I couldn't be more prepared. I had a swollen left ankle, a slight limp due to its stiffness, a sore toe on my right foot with a missing toe nail and two very sore heels to content with, so fit as a fiddle. Oh well not to worry, only 335 miles to go!

Awoke Sunday morning with a strange feeling in my gut. I got up knowing that this was the last time for a few weeks I would be sleeping in my own bed, which might not sound that weird but also away from the family for so long, something I'd never done before.

I'd booked a day return to London for the whole family. We were all going to spend the day together before parting later in the day to go our separate ways. Nothing Ann and the boys liked more than a trip into the city so when I suggested they travel up with me and spend the day up there, they didn't need a lot of encouragement.

What I didn't realise at the time was the Queen's birthday celebrations were going on so parts of London were extra busy and also some of the areas we liked to visit like St James's Park were partly cornered off.

First things first, when we got up to the city was to drop off my rucksack, the last thing I wanted to be doing was to be dragging it around all day, so straight onto the tubes and onto Blackfriars. I was staying at Blackfriars as this seemed to be the closest to St Paul's Cathedral.

Couldn't wait to get rid of my bag. It weighed a ton. We were a little bit early but I was able to check in. I do remember the assistants face on the check-in desk when I pulled out my paperwork all laminated.

*"Well, I've never seen anyone do that before,"* she said. Laminating my paperwork turned out to be a great idea. My paperwork managed to remain dry and crease free for the entire journey.

So checked in my bag, which was a great relief. Ann and the boys were very eager to move to other locations but first I had one more thing on the agenda. I wanted to familiarise myself with the area and my short route from the Inn to the Cathedral.

Once we were there a wanted to take a few snaps on the steps of the cathedral, a few with Ann and a few with the boys. Can't say I have my photo taken that often but I thought it would be a good idea to post a few pictures every day of my journey and how it was going.

Chores over and back on the tube and rest of the day hopefully relaxing with the family. To be quite honest it wasn't the cleverest of things to do, we actually clocked up a fair few miles that afternoon or should I say a lot.

With feet already feeling sore, I really should have had my feet up somewhere relaxing but it just wasn't to be. I can't remember every place we visited that afternoon but I do remember a few like Covent Gardens, Leicester Square, Hyde Park, Harrods, St James's Park and Trafalgar Square and not in the right order either.

We seemed to end up doing twice the miles we should have had we'd planned our day out properly. On a more positive note, mind I do remember sitting for a while in Hyde Park while the boys fed the squirrels.

It was Sunday, school the next day, so I didn't want the boys getting back too late and I'm guessing now but I think I went back with them to Paddington about 4pm or something like that. Got them straight onto a train that was sitting at one of the platforms.

There was about 10-15 minutes before the train left so I wondered back up to the main waiting area and then got myself back up to the platform in time to see their train depart and wave them off. It was literally from that moment onwards that reality was starting to sink in.

Got myself back onto the tubes and made my way back to Blackfriars. Suddenly, I was on my own! Family heading one way and me heading the other, an eerie feeling of loneliness and solitude. Time to think, time to reflect, no work tomorrow, no usual routine, no one to get up with, no one to chat to, no one to come home to at the end of the day.

Arrived at Blackfriars, got myself up to my room, shoes off, kettle on and wow I think it just hit me! The task ahead felt huge or to put it more frankly with the state of my feet already under strain and sore from missing skin and my painful toe, the task ahead felt humongous!

There was also the reality of having no choice. I'm not one for planning things much, more of a spur of the moment kind of guy. A good day out with the family would most often be a spur of the moment decision the evening before, as opposed to having it on the agenda for a week or more.

Here I was, task ahead of me imminent, I'd created it entirely myself and there was no way I could back track out of this one, couldn't even put it back a day if I wanted to. Mentally although a bit apprehensive, largely due I think to the state of my feet, I was as mentally prepared as I could ever possible be.

I lead a pretty busy life usually and with work, other commitments and family life it's rare I ever get the chance nowadays to sit down and reflect. Now I was about to get all the time in the world to do just that. Some ME time 24 hrs/day.

Spoke to Ann and the boys, made sure they were back home safely then decided to pop out round the corner. I remembered clocking a store earlier like a Tesco's Metro or something like that, so popped out to get some milk for tea and a few supplies for tomorrow like water. Didn't want to get my head down too late so once back I got myself down to the restaurant for dinner.

Restaurant looked pretty dam busy but I was thinking a table for one would surely be easy to find. I still remember very well where I was sitting, a cramped up little table with as much leg room as a cheap airline ticket and a great view of the back of someone's head or the wall.

Clientele around me all of a certain criteria, senior citizens or mature couples, sitting relaxing and knocking back the odd glass of wine or ten! I felt like a square peg in a round hole. My phone kept bleeping as I was receiving loads of text from friends, wishing me best wishes for my journey. Between receiving and sending text, I barely had time to eat my food. I remember the stares I was getting from nearby tables, classed as one of those younger generation dudes that sit with their fingers permanently attached to their phones.

I put it on silent to pacify them not that it had anything to do with them. Most of them were a damn site louder than my phone and that was before they'd had a drink! I wasn't sitting asking them to be silent.

Paid for my food, got back up to my room, finished a few texts and done one last thing. I logged on to my webpage where people could donate directly. I was chuffed to bits to find that a good friend of mine had made a decent donation and as I worked it out it took my grand total so far above the three grand mark.

I found it real strange the way different people reacted to donating. As I said before I learnt a lot about myself but also so much about others. There were many people that I would have naturally expected to donate that didn't, then there were a few true friends that donated far beyond what I would have ever expected.

There were complete strangers that donated that overwhelmed me with their generosity too. There were friends and acquaintances that I would have banked on helping me out but never gave a sausage! Or the ones that would tell you every time you see them but never quite getting round to doing it in reality.

Human nature's a funny old thing and when it comes down to money it couldn't get any weirder, I can tell you. Anyway, final preparations, satnav on charge, phone on charge, clothes out ready for the morning, quick chat with Ann and the boys then alarm set. First big day tomorrow, breakfast was to start at 6am, so set the alarm for 5:30am, then time to crash!

# Chapter 6
# Long First Day

Awoke by my alarm and got up, if I remember about 5:45am. Well, big day today; this is where it all began, no turning back now. Eager to get on this morning, quite excited, months of preparation and it was finally here. Got down to breakfast, I was the first down, I had to wait for them to let us in.

Had the usual Premier Inn breakfast, in and out as quick as I could, wanted to get on the road by 7:00 am. Back up to my room, teeth, toilet, charity bib on, bag on back, stick in one hand and in the other, a small mini sports bag type holdall.

I had brought this little Nike bag along with me as I thought it would be a pain to keep taking the rucksack off my back every time, I needed something out of it like a sip of water or to check the satnav, etc.

Anyway, so I handed in my room keys and with a positive mind-set, couldn't wait to set off, out into that crisp morning air and onto those busy London streets. Bagshot, here I come! With just a little over 31 miles ahead of me, I was as keen as mustard to get going.

First things first, back into that little Metro store to pick up lunch for the day. Not having a fridge back at the Inn, I was reluctant to pick something up the night before.

On from there and the first stop just had to be St Paul's Cathedral. It was actually putting me out of my way ever so slightly but just had to start from there, just as planned. I remember taking a few more snaps at the time from outside the Cathedral ready to post on to Facebook later that evening.

Walked right up to the steps of the cathedral and to my surprise the doors were already open, I guess I'm just so used to the lazy old town of Newbury where at 7:00am in the morning, there's not a lot you'd find open, in fact the majority of people would probably only just of got out of their beds.

Had to touch the Cathedral before I set off but it seemed such a shame not to pop inside and take a look, given that the open doors seemed to be beckoning me in. So, I walked up the steps and took myself inside. Just a quick peep I thought, just a brief moment to get a feel of where I was starting from and what task lay ahead, a bit of a reality check.

As I climbed the steps and made my entrance, I was greeted by two stocky security men. They acknowledged me invitingly but their body language was saying differently. Their eyes glued to me head to foot.

*"You're welcome to come in,"* one said *"but we'll have to check your bags."*

Well as much as I would have loved to have gone right inside and had a quick look around I really, really couldn't be bothered with going through all hassle of all that, besides I really did need to press on. I had a quick chat with them and told them what I was doing. I don't think they were really listening or understood but they were polite enough and wished me good luck!

Out from the Cathedral and onwards, towards the embankment. I had planned a route in my head to hit a few famous land marks on my way out of London. So straight towards the wobbly foot bridge, you know the one they had to attach some kind of shock absorber stabiliser things because people were so unhappy with the way the bridge was vibrating as they crossed it.

Along the embankment for a bit then turning off towards Trafalgar Square. Couldn't believe the number of bicycles along the route. First time I'd ever seen it but there were not just specialised cycle lanes but traffic lights for bikes as well.

I missed Trafalgar Square somehow; never mind I followed my nose as they say and got myself back on track cutting up through St James's Park and coming out onto The Royal Mall.

I was wondering the day before whether or not I would be able to do this part of the route or not because of all the coned off areas for the Queen's birthday celebrations but thankfully, everything had been reopened. I mean there were still hordes of barriers waiting around to be collected but at least it was all passable once again.

Walked up The Mall, straight up to Bucking Palace, quick cup a tea with the queen, *'of course'* then down the side and on towards Hyde Park Corner. Crossing the huge roundabout at Hyde Park Corner I couldn't believe the sheer number of bicycles around at that time in the morning.

You stand there at the lights and they build up all around you on both sides of the road. Then when the lights change, all hell lets loose as they race towards you. It's amazing there aren't more crashes as they all race off in different directions against each other.

As a pedestrian, for a moment it was like being in the middle of a twenty-lane carriageway and so unpredictable too. Not so bad if they travelled in a straight line but no, it's just a mess. A mass of cyclists playing chicken with each other and you're stuck in the middle.

Well, I was glad I was doing this walk this way round. City walking doesn't really do much for me but knowing I would soon be out into the country and leaving these bustling city streets behind us was great and something positive to look forward to.

The paths were pretty busy in places with commuters which was to be expected and I knew that coming out of London on a Monday morning wouldn't necessarily be the fastest progress, especially with a stick in one hand and a large rucksack on my back and so many roads to cross and navigate but to be honest it wasn't really too bad.

It was exactly 8:30am when I passed the front of Harrods on the A4. Not that I was watching the time but I still have a text on my phone that I received from a good friend and work college of mine, Robert. He was wishing me well.

I remember texting back to say *'just passing Harrods'* then come a reply *'snob'*, I had to laugh to myself. I hadn't done bad considering I'd been into the cathedral as well. The next time I would hear from Robert would be Saturday evening just before Honiton.

Next place of interest I would be passing was The Natural History Museum. I was trying to take a few snaps on the way but I only had my phone so they weren't brilliant but still nice to keep as memories and of course to post on face book at the end of the day. I was also careful to bear in mind that I didn't want the battery to run flat before the end of the day.

The weather was sort of ideal, not too hot, not too cold and nice and dry until of course it decided I was having it all too easy. The clouds were building and it had been gradually getting darker and darker since I had set out.

Can't remember now if I had checked the forecast the night before but to be quite honest, it didn't really make a hoot of difference if I had. My plans were set, come rain or shine and nothing short of a hurricane or an earthquake would have stopped me.

Closing in on the Hammersmith Fly-over and I could feel a slight drizzle in the air. Well, if that was all it was going to amount to then I wasn't too bothered and of course I didn't actually walk across the fly-over, I don't think that's possible, to be honest and would be extremely dangerous.

I had some dangerous stretches ahead of us but if there was a safer route around something then I would surely be opting for it, that's assuming it wasn't taking me miles out of my way I mean.

So much traffic and fumes in the air. The rain was ever so gradually but ever so persistently getting heavier and heavier. I was hoping it was going to be just a quick shower but it's a dilemma you find yourself in, do you stop, go through all the hassle of getting your rucksack all unclipped and off your back, sort out all your waterproofs, get yourself kitted out and redressed all for the sake of a 5min shower or what if it wasn't just a quick shower.

I also had a waterproof cover to go over my rucksack as it was only water resistant to a point and the last thing, I wanted was a bag full of soaking wet belongings, not to mention the extra weight I'd be carrying if it were to all get wet.

So, I gave in, found somewhere convenient to stop and kitted myself out with my waterproofs. I was walking in a pair of jeans and a big pair of walking boots so putting my waterproof bottoms on was not something I wanted to be doing that often, so it was really a choice of deciding do I wear then today or not?

I slipped them on, I was glad I did as the rain had become quite heavy at this point. With water dripping from my hair and down my face I couldn't help but be thinking, what have I let myself in for?

I did have a hood on my waterproof jacket but it tended to restrict your vison slightly and with being in such a built-up area with so many roads to cross and vehicles turning, I felt more at ease with my hood down.

What I wasn't accounting for of course was how so extremely uncomfortable it become wearing my waterproof bottoms over the top of my jeans. My legs were heating up inside and feeling sticky and all bunged up and I just suddenly felt so much more restricted.

I had to get them off and fast. The problem was I was out in public alongside a very busy main road and stripping off here didn't really seem like much of a good option. I'd more than likely get arrested or worse still cause an accident or something!

Shortly after moving away from the Hammersmith fly-over I came across a small strip of parkland area on the westbound side. As I veered away from the main road, I could actually see a park bench which appeared to be half secluded and out of site of the main road, set down into some flower garden type area.

Couldn't believe my luck, so with no one around or close enough that I could see, I seized the opportunity. I got myself down to the bench, unloaded myself and speedily started to strip. Boots off, waterproofs off and then of course my jeans!

So, there I am stripped down to my underwear in a public park at about 9am on a Monday morning hoping of course to be quick enough not to be spotted, next to a busy London carriageway and only yards away from a public foot path and overlooking properties.

I slipped my waterproofs back on as hastily as I could, from now on I would be completing the rest of my walk just wearing my waterproofs, well at least I would see how I got on today. Legs felt so much freer and more comfortable but the downside of course was just a bit more weight on my back, like I really needed that!

The rain soon stopped and if I remember rightly, it was dry for the rest of the day. As I marched on towards to the Hogarth roundabout and on towards the Chiswick fly-over I already felt that I had accomplished some ground behind me. Starting out from pretty much the centre of London I was now on top of what I considered to be the gateway out of the city, it was soon to be all behind us.

I reckon it must have been close to 10 o'clock when I'd reached the fly-over as I was fairly peckish already, mind I had walking now for about three hours and pretty much nonstop.

I picked myself up a bacon roll in the garage below the fly-over, you never quite know when you're going to pass the next shop. That dark depressing walk below the M4 was one part of the walk I was more than keen to get behind me and as I branched off onto the A4 leaving the constant pounding of the M4 motorway traffic behind me I was more than a little pleased, it felt like breaking free. Still had the big main road alongside but the surrounding land not quite so oppressive and increasingly feeling a little more open.

I think it wasn't until I got past Staines when I passed the first green field of the day. I stopped for lunch somewhere around the Staines area, sat outside a garage on an old brick wall and had a bit of a break. Finding somewhere to stop when you want wasn't an option and sometimes it was just about grabbing an opportunity when you could.

Sitting down taking the weight off my feet was nice but getting up again was not so easy. I can't lie, my feet were beginning to feel a bit sore, my left ankle was still playing up and I was starting to feel the weight of my rucksack digging into my shoulders.

I had a fair few miles under my belt but my destination felt far from easy reaching distance. The satnav was a great tool to have with us, set on walking mode it not only gave us the reassurance I was still on route but also an estimated time of arrival.

This of course did not take into consideration any stops for refreshments or of course the load I was carrying. Keeping up with the estimated time of arrival was crucial on a long day and I can assure you it wasn't just a walk in the park!

Further down the road, I branched off the A4 and on to the A30, heading directly now towards my destination, Bagshot. The land around was getting more and more open as I marched on but the footpaths getting narrower. I was now walking alongside a dual carriageway and there was a very small strip of grass between the footpath and the road.

This was all great while it lasted but by the time, I'd realised I'd made a big mistake it was too late! A few miles back where the carriageway started, I should have crossed over and walked the eastbound side so I was facing the traffic, for the path I was following sort of came to an end. It didn't actually end but with no prior warning decided to veer off away from the main road.

Now I might be mad but I'm not insane and to continue along the kerbside with my back to the oncoming traffic just wasn't an option. I could have kicked myself as the path led away, not deviating much at this point but whether I would be able to re-join the carriageway further up was anybody's guess.

The answer soon became quite apparent. As the path continued the traffic noise gradually became fainter which was not a good sign. The path came to an abrupt T-junction. Left was surely not the right direction as clearly it was never going to re-join the carriageway so I took a right in the hope it crossed to the other side of the road which would put me right back on track.

Unfortunately, this soon turned out to be a complete waste of effort, yes it did cross underneath the main road but on the other side I haven't a clue where it would have led me. I turned back and chose the other route. In my head I knew that although it was not following the main road, I may at least be able to cut across from here and pick up the route again further up.

I knew that where the A30 hit the M25 I would be turning left and following alongside the M25 for about a mile and then back onto the A30 towards Bagshot. So, I was pretty much following my nose now and trying to keep my bearings on the A30 in the distance. I knew I had to somehow cross the M25 and if I could just find my way to Egham I could get back on track.

With sore feet and aching back turning back was not an option, neither was losing my way! The path seemed to get narrower and narrower and more and more overgrown all the time. I had no choice but to keep following it.

In the distance, I could see a middle-aged woman coming towards me with her two dogs. Surely this had to be my opportunity for directions, she had to be local, very local I'd say. As we got closer and closer, she had no choice but to stop and stand aside in towards the bushes. To be quite honest it would have been very difficult for me with the size of my rucksack on my back and the size of the alley.

You could see the cautious look in her eyes as I approached, looking twice the size of her with my baggage and big stick in my hand as I strutted along. She may have had her two dogs with her but that seems to mean nothing nowadays, there are so many nutty people around. She made eye contact with me.

*"Afternoon,"* I said.

*"Afternoon,"* she replied.

*"You couldn't tell me how to get back to the A30, could you or over to the M25?"*

To be quite honest she didn't have a clue, she was about as useful as a chocolate teapot. Her dogs were pretty well behaved but a little agitated and why wouldn't they be. They were just doing what dogs do naturally, protecting her. So, I said good day to her, thanked her for her help and carried on my way.

About quarter of a mile further up, I met an old man. He wasn't much help either but he did at least tell me to stick to the path and it would soon lead me out to a main road, which was kind of helpful.

I remember crossing a railway line and sure enough I was soon back on the tarmac, half relieved to be clear of these doggy alleyways but I now had to get my bearings. Fortunately, I have a pretty good built-in sense of direction and I chose wisely.

Before I knew it, I was crossing beneath the M25, not exactly where I'd liked to have been heading but heading back towards the M25 /A30 junction from the other side. So, I'd been taken out of my way slightly but at least now I was sure to be back on route.

Going out your way slightly by car is one thing but when you're on foot, with a load on your back and given the distance I was walking that day, any distance out of your way was just mentally crippling as well as physically. I was sure never to make that same mistake again for the rest of my walk.

There was a short section of the A30 that runs alongside the M25 here and it really did feel like a no walk zone. I mean I know I was technically on an A road but it felt more like walking an eight-lane carriageway of the M25.

There was no proper pathway so I just kept over as tight as I could. The small Nike bag I had brought with me was black and illuminous green. Although carrying it along was a pain in the arse sometimes it turned out to be a blessing at times like this.

I would dangle it down in my left hand and push it out slightly at any approaching traffic, not enough to startle anyone but just enough to alert on coming drivers of my presence. I gradually got it off to a fine art during the course of my walk in the days that followed.

I was soon away from the M25 and yet again this felt like I'd achieved a great milestone. Evening rush hour was now pretty much upon us but by memory I think I had a footpath the rest of the way. It was a very boring straight road ahead and I was beginning to feel a bit weary.

This first day had been really testing for me and my ETA seemed to be getting further and further away as my pace gradually slowed. My bag was killing me and my thoughts were turning to making my load lighter.

I couldn't see a practical way forward as it was; I mean the straps were looking pretty strained and I was even wondering if the bag was going to last the journey carrying so much weight, let alone my own physical capability. I had to do something and fast, giving up now was simply not an option.

The last few miles seemed endless. I remember reaching Sunningdale. I was familiar with this small place as it was once the home of one of my bosses' years ago. When I say home, it wasn't where he was from as I'm sure if I remember right his mother lived on Tyneside.

On my way through, I called in to a local grocery/newsagent store as I was gasping for a drink and a bit of energy like a chocolate bar or something just to get us by for the last few miles. The prices were absolutely ridiculous, now I don't mind paying over the top and to be honest, you kind of expect that in a small store but to be completely taken the micky out of was against my principles completely.

I guess local people round there had too much money to waste but I wasn't going to encourage him. I had a dribble of water left and I dug deep into my bag for a protein bar, I may have already have had today's quota but I could always replace them. I had another quick stop; my legs were killing me.

I staggered back to my feet and got myself going again. Oh course, I would have to be stopped by the level crossing, that's always inevitable, sods law as they call it. As I trudged the last few miles to the Inn, I was sure it was the weight in my bag that was crippling me, if I could simple loose a few pounds it could make all the difference.

I had two options I could think of. One was to call my parents. They lived in Slough, not far from Bagshot, so if they were to meet me at the Inn, I could off load some weight to them. Alternatively, I could get my wife to meet me the next evening at Basingstoke, the next day was one of my shortest stretches.

The first option would seem the most practical, another day carrying that load was not something I was really looking forward to, plus of course my wife does not drive so the second option wasn't really ideal. The only other option was to ask the hotel to look after a bag of my belongings and I would collect them at a later date.

As I closed in on the Inn, I was beginning to feel a great sense of relief. Counting down the yards on my satnav, then to see that Premier Inn sign ahead, it felt like all my birthdays had come at once I dragged myself into the reception and collapsed in a chair while I sorted my paperwork. Sod's law again.

My room was up the stairs, along a corridor, then along another corridor, I don't think they could have found me a room much further away if they tried! I threw my stuff on the floor, pulled my boots from my feet and collapsed on the bed.

Freedom for my feet and no weight on my back felt so good. Kettle on then on the phone, I'd convinced myself the best and most practical option was to call my parents. They seemed more than happy to help out and were soon on their way over.

I jumped in a nice hot bath to try to relax my body then set about going through my belongings meticulously trying to work what had to stay and what had to go! My first aid had to stay; I'd already whittled this down to the bare essentials before I set off.

I must say I was so relieved to have some decent muscle rub in my bag as my shoulders and back really did feel a bit punished.

My parents turned up, I met them at the reception and took them up to my room. I had all my gear laid out on the bed. They couldn't believe the amount of gear I was carrying. I unloaded my spare pair of boots, my spare satnav, a pair of socks, from today and a couple of t-shirts and the bottoms I'd set out in at the start of the day as I'd made up my mind, I would just wear my waterproof bottoms from now on.

I just remembered, they weren't jeans, they were a canvas type trouser that I'd been wearing but nevertheless I would be doing away with them from now on. My spare satnav I could afford to lose as I was now happy my primary one had lasted the whole day, plus of course I always had my phone for a backup if I got desperate.

My boots of course I just hoped to God I was never going to need them and this was a risk I was going to have to take, I mean why would a perfectly good pair of walking boots fail but in the back of my mind remembering where I'd bought them and how much I'd paid?

That small amount of weight out of my bag seemed to make a fair bit of difference. My bag now almost felt comfortable and the straps not quite so strained. I was confident that this was just all first day teething problems and all would be ok from now on.

I must admit my feet already felt fairly sore so I smothered them in Sudocrem and placed them in plastic food bags before putting my socks back on. I had a few hours yet before I set off again in the morning so I was confident they would recover nicely. I know how good Sudocrem can be on a baby's bum so if it could do that magic on their tender skin the surely my feet would be a doodle.

Sat in the restaurant again with my phone bleeping away. Might sound a bit unappreciative but all I wanted to do was sit and relax and do nothing but I felt compelled to send back a few massages from text I'd received during the day.

Stopping earlier wasn't really an option, with time against me and weariness getting the better of me, all I wanted to do was to keep pushing myself on. Stopping, then pulling out my glasses to return a message and then having to get going again wasn't really ideal.

71

When your feet are aching that much the moment you stop, they begin to seize up, then it was twice as hard to get going again. Bear in mind I hadn't been walking quite as I should have been thus putting strain on other parts of my feet.

Got up to my room, had a quick chat with Ann and the boys, then decided to call it a day. Just couldn't believe how hard today had been. It was never supposed to be like this, not at all! This was my first day, still had 300 miles to go! Thank God I've always been an optimist!

# Chapter 7
# Boots, Here We Come!

Up early again today, down to the restaurant first thing, grabbed myself a decent breakfast, then back up to my room for final preps' before I set off. I did have a few routines that I had to get myself used to.

Every morning I had to remember my tablets, ibuprofen for my left foot to help stop the swelling and my hay fever tablets as I would spend a lot of time walking amongst the bushes on the road side or weeds should I say.

To be quite truthful, I rarely take tablets at home as I believe your body must eventually get used to them and become less effective but right now, I needed them. Likewise with the hay fever tablets, I wouldn't usually take them but I must admit they seemed incredibly effective and they were only really cheap ones from Wilkinson's if I remember.

So, keys handed in and back out into the fresh morning air. Bit of a shorter day today, next stop Basingstoke so only had just over 20 miles to cover. Unfortunately, the fresh morning air didn't seem to last long.

As I strolled or marched should I say along the roadside of the A30, rush hour traffic was building and I just remember walking past miles of queuing traffic, well it seemed like miles? With the air heavy with petrol and diesel fumes it was just as well I wasn't asthmatic!

My bag felt a bit more comfortable today. I was probably carrying about 13 kilos plus water, a fair load but not quite as pressing as it was. I think today's route was one of the most boring routes of the whole trip.

I basically set off from the Inn on the A30, then followed the A30, then a bit more A30, then more A30, then more A30, in fact the whole walk was down the A30. So other than checking my progress for time, my satnav today was pretty much not needed.

I was on a mission today, only one thing on my mind. This was one of the few locations that I would be stopping right next to a town centre and with the added fact that I had such a short distance today, if you can call 20 miles a short walk.

I was on a mission to get to the shops before they closed. My feet were still pretty sore and I was desperate to get to Boots to get some gel insoles or something like that to help them.

I remember a fair distance of the walk was initially quite urbanyfied, if that's a word. I remember walking through Blackwater and stopping at a local store to get some supplies. I recognised the area as I'd recently done a job nearby. Don't ask me how I got to do a job in Blackwater but it's a bit of a long story through connections and acquaintances over the years.

On from Blackwater and the footpaths disappeared. A fair long stretch of dual carriageway lay ahead and this became my first real long stretch of road walking. Feet pretty much killing me and my little toe so painful to walk as it pushed against the inside of my boots that my walk had turned into some kind of twisted limp.

I'd plastered up my little toe and bombarded it with antiseptic cream over the last couple of days for the fear that there may be an infection setting in. It was painful enough just to touch so the last thing I needed was an infection getting where the nail had failed.

Awkwardly walking or limping along, I pressed on regardless, hell bent on reaching Basingstoke in good time. This was my one chance of getting access to some essential emergency care products plus hopefully a well-earned rest before commencing a mammoth stretch, I had lined up for the following day.

I did actually reach the Basingstoke Premier Inn at about 2:30pm and collapsed in the chair in the reception yet again. The feeling of successfully reaching my destination yet again mentally uplifting but couldn't wait to get my boots off. Checked in then up to my room where I literally tossed my gear aside and lay on the bed, tired out with feet tingling in pain.

Conscious of the time, I dragged myself into a nice deep hot bath. With blisters now appearing in several locations and the sheer soreness of my heels, jumping into a hot bath was simply not an option. It was more of a case of gradually introducing my feet bit by bit to the temperature.

There would usually be other body parts that I would consider before subjecting myself to a steaming hot bath but not today. Well, it comes to something when your feet are more sensitive than your nuts, doesn't it!

Not sure if I really needed a hot bath or a cold bath but the heat certainly seemed to ease my legs and back. I desperately needed to get over to the town centre so I didn't spend too long bathing. To be honest it was just as well. I had good reason to get out as I could have quite easily fallen asleep in there.

My walk down into the town centre was quite a slow one. Every step I took was painful. Between my sore heels and my painful toe, there was no real comfortable way of placing down my right foot and my left foot just wouldn't bend properly at the ankle. So, I staggered along with the help of my stick, destination Boots the Chemist.

Would have to be right across the town wouldn't it, right through the inside precinct then out the other side and up through the outside one. At least my trip wasn't in vain as I found a super pair of gel soles for my feet and a few more deep heat products for my back and legs.

Very close by to Boots was KFC, all too irresistible to turn down, mind had it not been on route and with the state of my feet, I would have thought differently. The seating area in this one is upstairs but didn't fancy climbing the stairs, taking the lift looked very tempting.

There were children playing around in the front of the store. They were messing around with the lift, it was one of those disabled ones for wheelchairs and push chairs, etc. Back when I was their age, if you would have been doing what they were doing, you would have got a clip round the ear or the security man would have ushered you out the shop.

Nowadays, it would seem that people are too afraid to say anything to them. They should have known better, they weren't that young, they were basically young adults on their way home from school. Shame they didn't act their age really. Had I been in a better frame of mind, I would have probably said something to them myself. I took the stairs in the end as I wasn't in the mood for confrontation.

Sainsbury's was more or less opposite so after KFC I popped into the store for some milk and a few other bits. I half bumped into a chap in there who was asking for directions to Premier Inn, which was not the easiest place to give directions for from where we were.

When I say half bumped into him, what I mean is he was asking somebody next to me and I overheard. I did my best to explain to him exactly where it was plus mentioned to him that I was heading back there myself but best not wait for me, that was if he wanted to make it back by midnight with the speed I was walking.

I wasn't exactly walking at much of a pace but I was fully aware that the sooner I did get back, the more time my feet would have to recover. Had a big day looming tomorrow, destination Salisbury. I'm sure the guy would have found it ok, I'm not usually bad at giving directions.

Wasn't really ready to eat properly when I got back but I booked a table in the restaurant for later just in case it got busy. Had a bit of time before dinner so I set about sorting out the gel soles I'd bought. They were made in one size and marked out with different foot sizes to be cut down to fit.

I had a small or very small, should I say, pair of scissors in my kit, I'd brought for cutting small plasters and bandages. Thought I'd check them out and see if they were man enough for the job. Well, they were about as good as toothless baby chewing on a ropy bit of steak.

I doubt to be honest they could have cut through butter; they were just folding sideways. Next idea was a sharp pair of nail clippers but yet again absolutely useless, what the hell do they make them things with, everything just seems to bounce back off them.

I was desperate to get these soles fitted, I didn't just buy them to sit and tease me and they weren't cheap either. I was going to get them cut if I had to rip them apart with my teeth.

Somewhere on the premises there had to be a decent pair of scissors, so I made my way back down to the reception. The same guy was there from earlier when I checked in. I explained my predicament, not knowing what his response was going to be but he was very accommodating and not finding a pair in his desk he set off to see what he could find.

He returned with a gleaning pair of scissors in his hands, it was like waving an ice-cream in front of a small child. I'd left my boots upstairs but had already worked out which line to cut. I sat in reception and cut out what I hoped to be the perfect size.

I was most grateful to the gentleman's help, handed back the scissors then trudged back up to my room to check out the fit. They were perfect! Or at least as good as they were going to be.

Feet still really sore, I went down to the restaurant in my socks that evening, felt like a bit of a chav really but when needs must and just hoped they wouldn't mind. Turned out the restaurant was really quiet so all that baloney about having to book was really just their old sales spill.

Had a pretty relaxing evening, this was my longest rest I'd have, from now on the days were about to get longer and longer. Seemed a bit strange having done all the miles I'd done so far yet only being in Basingstoke, a town I was so familiar with only a few miles up the road from where I lived in Newbury.

In a weird sort of way, I had a feeling of not getting very far or should I say not accomplishing much ground. I'd travelled so far yet I was still so close to home.

After going back up from dinner, I put my feet up and relaxed and done everything I could to prepare myself for the next day. Smothered my feet in Sudocrem, bombarded my little toe in antiseptic cream and smothered my body in muscle relief wherever it felt stressed like my back and legs and shoulders.

My room must have stank of deep heat, so I felt a bit guilty for anyone staying in my room the next evening. I know they have rules on taking smelly food into your room like garlic and smelly curries and things but I'm not sure they have any rules about medical products, well not that I'm aware.

Not a fan of the TV, never have been in fact, so finished the evening off listening to a radio channel, relaxing on my bed just chilling out. With my alarm set for an early rise again, I settled down quietly, optimistic that tomorrow would be a better day. Well, it had to be didn't it!

# Chapter 8
# The Storm

Wednesday 15<sup>th</sup> June. Woke up early that morning as usual. Got my head down at a reasonable time the night before and woke up in a great positive frame of mind, I knew I had a tough day ahead of me today. Destination today, Salisbury, just a casual 36 miles away or near enough.

This was my longest stretch, I had put a lot of thought into these distances when planning this walk and whether I'd been a bit over optimistic or not, well it was too late to worry about that now, I just had to get on with it!

Surely my feet would be better this morning they'd had a nice long rest and pampered the night before with some TLC, I now had one hell of a day ahead of me, so they just had to be! Not sure it was a day ahead of me, felt more like a day and half by the time it was over.

Could things get any worse I wondered, well of course they could, by the end of the day, things were looking pretty ugly for me!

So, I sat up in my bed, drew back the covers and placed my feet slowly onto the floor. As I gradually increased the weight onto the soles of my feet, I could tell instantly that things were not 100% despite the rest I'd had, I think I was a little over optimistic on my speed of recovery.

I'm not saying they were unbearable but they were far from comfortable. Hopefully just the initial shock of putting some weight back down on them. I put a few plasters over a few blisters to ease the friction and wrapped up my little toe.

I decided to go down to breakfast in my walking boots, I knew that easing my feet back into my boots might be painful but I really didn't want to go down to the restaurant in my socks and feel like a right chav again. Plus of course, if I was going to have to wear these boots anyway, it was a chance of getting used to them before setting off again.

So I slowly edged my feet inside the boots. I could have sworn they weren't the same boots I set off in, somebody must of shrank them or something or stolen them and replaced them with another pair two sizes smaller, as they felt tighter around my toes than ever before. I guess it must have been the swelling that was making them feel tighter.

Mind I must admit with the new gel soles underfoot, I did at least feel some added comfort as I stood up and walked across the room. If only my toe was not in pain, I could have screamed at it.

I felt like ripping the damn thing out of its socket and discarding it or cutting the front of my boots off and turning them into some kind of open toe boots like a pair of boots cum sandals.

Popped down to the restaurant, had breakfast and got out as soon as I could. Now I really couldn't afford to hang around today, I had one hell of a stretch to do. So out of the Inn as quick as I could and raring to go, well sort of!

Mentally all I wanted to do was to march down the road at a stonking pace and leave Basingstoke behind me in a flash but in reality, no it wasn't that simple, so, so frustrating as I set off down the road at a pace that was far from adequate.

With the pain in my feet, it was a case of setting off at a slow pace and gradually building up speed. It was like having to walk them in to get them going again.

Got myself up to a reasonable pace, still limping mind but just had to keep moving forward. Out of Basingstoke and into the countryside! Hadn't got far out of town if I remember when I came across a very narrow arched bridge type tunnel, so narrow in fact that pedestrians were forbidden to pass.

I could clearly see the other side but not being able to see around the approaching bend walking through would have been like playing Russian roulette with the traffic. With nowhere to escape for a brick wall on both sides ignoring this warning sign was not an option.

The path itself seemed to veer off at a funny angle and after already being caught out once between Staines and Egham I was very apprehensive about following it but what choice did I have? As it goes the detour turned out to be quite small, which was a relief. If I remember rightly, I was on the B3400.

I really did feel like I was now right out in the countryside as the roads seemed somewhat narrower in general to what I'd walked so far. As I pressed on further the footpaths became very narrow and in places more often than not became non-existent.

I do remember some footpaths that were there but not there, they were sort of useable, you had to have your wits about you for the hedgerows with wild flowers and brambles, nettles and long grasses and weeds were so overgrown they were up to face height in places and even above my head.

I think if I remember rightly, it was some new government excuse, I mean 'policy', not to cut back the verges so as to preserve the wildlife. Nothing at all to do with cut backs off course, excusing the pun, honestly!

Have you tried walking through the countryside nowadays? They keep banging on about keeping fit, walking or running and not just sitting in front of a computer screen for entertainment but have you seen the state of the countryside. I think they need to rewrite the maps.

If you're thinking of planning a walk these days, I suggest you try to stick to the main footpaths only unless you're prepared to carry a sickle, a decent pair of pruners or a chain saw even and a good first aid kit! And no, it's not my poor map reading skills, I've often been out on short country walks with the family and yes, we were in the right location but the footpaths have virtually disappeared.

There can be nettles head high, dilapidated stiles and even stiles and openings sealed off where cheeky farmers try their best to deter the public from walking the land.

Anyway, so getting back to what we were talking about. There at your feet, somewhere, would be a foot wide strip of tarmac, so overgrown, the edges as straight as an old man's set of teeth, just about visible through the undergrowth.

Walking along was a real effort in places and quite hazardous, pushing back the tall stems with your stick and trying not to go arse over tip as the stronger ones tangled round my already crippled feet.

Glad I took the hay fever tablet as this was a real test for it as I'm sure my eyes would have been streaming by now. I really did feel like I was right in the country yet funny enough not that far from home but then again Newbury is quite rural as it's surrounded by countryside anyway.

The hedge rows were quite pretty in places, messy but natural and loaded with beautiful foxgloves and daisies and other white and yellow wild flowers, broken up in places with beautiful red poppies and blue cornflowers. Not an expert on wild flowers but I could name a few.

One thing that I didn't bargain on was the sheer amount of road walking that I'd be doing. I talked about getting a decent pair of boots in my preparations, fully expecting to have to walk miles and miles of roadside verges with miles of uneven ground beneath my feet but what I didn't account for was the sheer pain I would be in trying to walk the rugged land.

The problem wasn't so much as what you could feel through the side of your boots, I mean it wasn't like the princess and the pea but more to do with not being able to place my foot down flat. As my feet became more and more sensitive to step down, being able to control how I placed them down became essential for pain management.

Plus of course with the way my feet were starting to feel and the weight on my back, walking these uneven verges made it so much more likely for me to trip and with such narrow verges in places, this could have been disastrous.

I passed on through the little village of Overton. I recognised it from one of the practise walks Matt had done while walking with his school. The route was pretty straight and seemingly endless in places and although quite pleasant did get a bit monotonous at times.

I remembered counting the miles down as I edged towards Whitchurch, a very small town I was familiar with and was looking forward to having a proper break when I got there. I knew there were shops ahead for some supplies and I was eager to reach them. It's amazing how long a mile can seem when you're counting down your steps.

Arrived in Whitchurch in pretty good time and was chuffed to bits to see a most welcoming bench sitting right outside the Co-op store, smack bang on route too. So, into the Co-op to pick up some lunch. I hadn't had a chance to pick anything up yet but always knew there was a shop here when I set off, so wasn't too concerned.

One of the things you quickly got use to was not to miss an opportunity when you got one. You could literally walk miles and miles between shops and garages and at times even finding somewhere to stop for a quick drink break was a problem. Took my rucksack off my back and carried it round the store.

The isles were quite narrow so I didn't want to look like a bull in a China shop and wreck half the joint on my way round. Picked myself up some sandwiches, one for now and one for later, got some other bits too, maybe a bottle of Lucozade for some extra energy and usually some kind of chocolate bar, typically a Snickers or something like that with nuts in, a good source of energy for walking.

You could tell the store had a very locally feel about it, the staff seemed very chatty with the customers. You could sense that proper village feel. With my rucksack in one hand and stick in the other, with my brightly coloured bib I was wearing with the charity name splashed all over it, my hiking boots on and me doing a balancing act with the stick and the bits I was buying, it was pretty obvious to the lady behind the till, that I was doing some kind of charity event.

"*Have you come far?*" she asked.

"*Basingstoke,*" I replied.

"*That's a fair way,*" she said.

"*Where are you heading?*"

"*Salisbury today,*" I replied.

She seemed quite taken back and we had a quick chat about what I was doing. She was keen to put one of my leaflets up in the store, now I don't want to sound ungrateful but, in some ways, this was a pain as I had to dig down right to the bottom of my sack and pull a few out but I couldn't miss the opportunity.

If only one person would have made a donation, to me it would have been worth it. I'd brought a few leaflets with me, yes, I know it was all extra weight but bear in mind the whole reason I was doing this walk was to raise money for this wonderful cause, so it seemed to make sense to me to be able to pass details on to people whenever I came across somebody who wanted to donate.

I sat outside the Co-op, took the weight off my feet for a good 5 to 10 minutes while I sat and had my sandwiches and rehydrated myself too. Instead of keeping buying water, I'd keep old bottles and refill them at the Inn from the tap. I could have sat there all day I can tell ya but needs must and I just had to crack on!

So back up onto my feet, rucksack on back and off I set again. Every time I stopped, my feet and legs would seem to seize up a little bit more so those initial few steps were always an effort to get going. I didn't actually get far before I realised, I was missing something important.

I'd left my stick inside the shop. It must have been when I put my stick down to rummage through my rucksack for those leaflets that I had placed it up against the counter then got side tracked and left it behind.

A few seconds of panic set in as for a very brief moment I had a vision of leaving it behind somewhere where I'd stopped for a sip of water or something before relieving myself with the assurance, I'd left it behind in the shop. Sure enough, it was there perched up against the counter just where I had left it.

So, I set off now heading directly towards Andover. I remember passing below the A34. Now the A34 runs virtually within a mile of my house just a few miles north of here so it seemed a bit strange again that I was so close to home. I guess this was the nearest I would ever get to passing my house as from now on at last, I could only be getting further away.

I was so glad of having that little green bag with me as there were paths ahead where the trees and bushes were kissing the roadside and long strips of tall hedges accompanied with dangerous bends in the road made for a dangerous place to be walking.

Made excellent time to Andover. Yet again it seemed strange as I passed right through the town centre, another local town to Newbury but the other direction this time. If I recall correctly, it was about 12:30 as I swept through the town.

I remember thinking to myself it would have been great to of met up with Ann on the way through and had a quick spot of lunch. She gets the bus over to Andover on the odd occasion, mind predicting what time I would have been passing through would have been a bit of a gamble.

I'd really been pushing on today, knowing how much ground I had to cover. I think the gel soles had made a huge difference to the comfort of my feet, mind still couldn't quite walk as I usually would thanks to my left ankle, my right little toe and my sore heels but I could limp along now at quite a pace, providing I was on flat ground. The day was certainly far from over with a good almost 16 miles still ahead of me.

So out of Andover and heading straight back towards the A30 to take me on to Salisbury. I was now back on a fast-moving main road with rarely a footpath to follow in places. The road now was a lot more bendythan it had been between Bagshot and Basingstoke and the land gradually becoming a lot hillier.

With cars now speeding towards us at crazy speeds and lorry and juggernauts thundering past it sure wasn't for the faint hearted.

The weather had been quite kind to me up until now but the clouds were now darkening all around and the distant sky becoming dirty looking and quite aggressive. Mother Nature was now stirring her stick and cooking something up to throw at me with all her might!

Storm clouds were building and rain was imminent. I could hear the sound of thunder rumbling away in the distance and the light was gradually fading as the dark clouds closed in on us. I found a convenient place to perch my gear as I kitted myself out for the inevitable.

Waterproofs on head to foot and rucksack now covered I pressed on into the storm. With thunder and lightning now surrounding me in every direction there I was miles from cover but so ready to endure the worst that could be unleashed on me. Mentally I was so prepared for this, this was always going to happen at some point, this is what we call enduring the great outdoor isn't it!

The rain started slowly drop by drop but then became heavier and heavier, the sky was loaded. As it made its assault from the heavens above there was me on the open road, a bit too open I might add and with the land now rolling up and down I was about to encounter something I hadn't foreseen.

Before I set off that morning, I'd done all my usual routines and prepared myself as best I could for the countryside and all its wild life within. Hay fever tablets being essential but of course that wasn't my only weapon against nature.

Not wanting to become part of the menu for every gnat, bug and beetle around, my wife had supplied me with sun protection with built in insect repellent. As I said before, she'd bought half of Boots the Chemist for us but I just took what I thought would be the essentials.

I didn't want the hassle of pulling along a trailer as well as my rucksack on my back. So anyway, before I'd set out today, I'd covered my face with this insect repellent stuff which was great by the way, it really did seem to be doing its job.

The problem was now as the rain was dripping down my face the cream was now running into my eyes, my hood was down as visibility was quite poor and conditions worsening. I'd sprayed insect repellent on my head as well and this was now running down my face and my eyes were now stinging like mad as I made my way squinting but still trying to watch where I was going as I struggled on.

Your eyes can be such a sensitive organ and mine even more so, not going to go into it now but a few years ago I had laser treatment on my eyes as I was suffering from Map Dot Corneal Dystrophy.

A condition that effects the cornea. I had an extremely thin layer of my cornea removed which was an excruciatingly painful procedure indeed, so with sensitive corneas, conditions were not good for me at all.

My feet were too sore now to walk on the verges, mind in places these verges did not now exist. There was often a small strip of tarmac between the edge of the road and the solid white line which marks out the edge of the lane for the traffic.

With lorries and cars still thundering past, headlights now on, my little green bag now vital. This small strip of tarmac was fast beginning to disappear as the flood waters started to build. Water was now cascading down the hills and the road side was readily becoming a shallow fast flowing torrent of water.

The road was gradually narrowing but the traffic reluctant to adhere to the atrocious conditions. The water just got deeper and deeper, becoming a lake at the side of the road. My choices were bleak, my answer was clear.

My choice was to either steer round the flood waters and walk miles out into the road directly into the path of the oncoming traffic or wade through the tides and endure the pounding of the spray and wash waters from the tyres cutting through close by. Need I say which option I choose!

My waterproofs were now being tested to their limits and my boots beyond that! The water was even deeper than I could have imagined and as I felt the coldness of the water filtering down on the inside of my boots, I had a sinking feeling in my stomach. My sore feet were now about to be punished beyond all reasonable endurance.

Too late now, the damage was done, my only hope now was to keep pushing forward to reach my destination as quickly and efficiently as possible and face the consequences later. I mean waiting for the flood waters to recede could have taken hours, time which I didn't have and walking around them would have been far too dangerous to contemplate.

My pace grew slower as the day went on. My calves stiff from the cold of the rain. The rain eventually cleared by and I considered trying to stop to put some dry socks on my feet but with the ground so soaking wet everywhere and damp there was nowhere to rest.

My boots were now so cold and damp and my feet so sore, trying to change my footwear would have been putting my feet through more pain than I wanted to chance right now. Every step now felt like one too many, stopping now became a real dilemma.

Stopping for water was essential but every time no matter how short, my feet and legs would start to cease and getting going again was such an effort. I was having to spray deep heat on my calves now just to stop then cramping up. Such an effort to keep pushing forward but my only hope of ending today's pain.

My mind was now going into pain management mood and subconsciously suppressing some of the physical stresses and strains now trying to engulf me. The route was now beginning to feel endless, my target time slowly slipping further and further away and every hill beginning to feel like a mountain.

As I came round one of the bends still some four or five miles from my destination, there in front of me, just across the road, two people were waving away at me, filming me as I hobbled along. Couldn't quite believe what I was seeing or who rather.

John and Patsy stone, the same guys I'd set up next to in Vicky Park the day of the Crafty Craft, the same guys I'd installed a kitchen for earlier this year. There they were filming me on their iPad, the last thing I needed right now was to break my pace or direction but I just had to stop to be polite, my body just wanted to keep moving or not rather, little did they know the pain I was in, if I stopped again now I was going to regret it.

I crossed over to greet them, shook their hands, hugged them then if I remember rightly, we took some snaps of us together. I was so grateful of their support; I just hoped the pain on my face wasn't saying otherwise. I must admit the thought did entre my mind having met these guys and having their car sitting there, the last few miles in a car would be great but there was no way I was asking.

I was determined to see this day through on my own esteem regardless to how I felt. Taking a lift would have felt like pure failure, falling at the first real hurdle or bottling out when the going got tough! That just wasn't me, never will be!

As I saw them off, I took the opportunity to rehydrate myself and plaster my legs with some more muscle rub to ease the discomfort. I inched away across the bumpy grass gradually picking up pace again.

The last few miles really did seem endless. Every hill I climbed I remember thinking over this summit and I'd be heading straight down towards Salisbury but the road ahead seemed to just tease me with one slope after another.

The rush hour was building or should I say under full swing. Twice, I had a driver stop and offer me a lift, I think partly because the people around there were so friendly and partly because road seemed so dangerous people were actually concerned for my safety.

Reassuring to know there are such lovely people around, I hated stopping even for a brief moment but it warmed the heart to know that peopled cared. One man that stopped, dark man, he actually passed us on the other side of the carriageway, gone past and turned round to come back to me, he stopped me and asked me if I needed a lift.

Then when I explained why I had to walk, he reached into his pocket and handed me a twenty-pound note, what a smashing guy, he'd brought the traffic to a complete stop behind him and I was preparing for the horns and the fist waving to follow but no, not today.

Believe it or not, not everyone is quite so polite as I found out during the course of my walk. This chap however was a great example of human kindness and compassion and along with other events like bumping into John and Patsy and being offered a lift into town my spirits were high as I did the final push of the day. I remember actually counting down the last few yards on my satnav.

As I hobbled into the Inn, it really was mind over matter as my legs gave way beneath me as I crashed into a waiting chair in the small reception room. I still remember that moment vividly in my mind, I pulled the rucksack from my back desperate to dig out some supplies.

I felt completely dehydrated and my heart was pounding and my head was spinning! I didn't feel right at all, I'd pushed myself beyond all expectations. My mind had taken over some miles back and my body had been running on pure adrenalin and determination.

I'd exhausted myself of all energy and drained my resources almost to the point of collapse. I think I drank a full litre of water nonstop and refuelled with a Snickers and an energy bar or whatever came to hand. I sat for a while and regained my senses.

I pulled the boots from my feet; my socks were still soaking. My heart rate came down and my head stopped spinning, I realised I'd pushed myself dangerously too far that day. I learnt a valuable lesson of keeping on top of my water intake on a more regular basis.

I'd abused myself for the sake of not stopping more regularly. I always knew today was going to be a tough one with the distance I was covering but just never contemplated just how tough!

My feet were killing me and I couldn't wait to get to my room, strip off and soak in a deep bath. Even standing up at the reception desk felt like a real challenge for me that day. The lovely lady behind the desk was so nice, she even carried my bags to my room for me as I shuffled behind her inch by inch down the corridor.

I crashed out on the bed, peeled the socks from my feet. I couldn't believe the state of my feet. Trench foot I think they call it, my skin was all wrinkled and sore like I'd spent too long in the bath, there were big flaps of skin hanging off and huge blisters and red friction marks around my ankles where my wet socks had taken their toll rubbing away at my softened skin in my boots.

Yet again, I had to be really careful in the bath as placing my feet directly into the hot water would have been too much to bear. My feet needed a rest and my stomach needed refuelling but after bathing my feet, they were in no fit state to carry me down to the restaurant just yet.

I covered them in Sudocrem as thick as I could and covered them completely up right past my ankles with a roll of cling film, I had brought with me. I also spent a fair while with a hairdryer heating up my boots in an attempt to dry them out. I needed them dry for the morning plus my socks needed drying out as well.

Yes, I had clean dry socks to wear but the last thing I needed was the added weight of wet clothes to carry. My room was a complete tip where I'd just throw stuff out from my bag and spread the contents across the floor and over the bed. The last thing on my mind was keeping my room tidy, I can assure ya!

I eventually dragged myself down to the restaurant, with a pair of open toed sandals in one hand and stick in the other, I shuffled myself down through reception and out through the front door. You needed to go out and back in again to get to the restaurant at the Salisbury branch. Now socks and sandals is something that I would never do as I never intended to wear my socks in the evening.

Neither did I ever have visions of needing my stick to get me to dinner but walking now was so painful, I had no choice. The restaurant was quiet and I apologised to the staff for not wearing my shoes. They were absolutely fine about it, well put it this way, they didn't seem to make a fuss.

Couldn't believe just how tough today had worked out. There I was, now just three days into my walk and the best part of 90 miles under my belt. I don't think my feet could have been in a worse state than they were yet I still had no thoughts of jacking in what so ever.

All I could think of was how much pain I was going to be in tomorrow if my feet hadn't heeled overnight. I guess I really was hoping for miracles and taking my optimism to the extreme. Tomorrow was no walk in the park either with over 30-mile trek ahead of me to Frome. I could have cursed that storm. A mean if my feet weren't struggling enough already the storm had just finished them off completely!

Spoke to Ann and the boys like I had done every evening. I'm sure she could tell in my voice I wasn't happy with the way things were going and the pain in my voice would have been evident. I'd had some real high points today but the low points were just smothering them and keeping a positive state of mind was becoming harder all the time.

# Chapter 9
# The Guilt!

Thursday 16<sup>th</sup> June. Up early, room still a tip! Needed to get myself organised. Needed to sort my bag, my tablets, teeth and of course the water, every morning I'd prepare fresh water in the plastic bottles I'd accumulated. This wasn't just so I didn't have to keep buying it but you never could tell when you were going to pass the next shop for supplies, so carrying plenty of water was essential.

I also had the added task now of wrapping my feet in cling film, I'd removed the cling film from the night before, before settling down, so as to get some air to my feet. I now had to decide whether to wrap them up again in the hope it would ease the pain walking.

Mind Sudocrem wasn't the answer for this, I had another trick up my sleeve, I'd brought along a small amount of Vaseline. Before I set off for my walk, I'd read about how Vaseline could ease the friction on your skin, so time to put it to the test!

In an ideal world, I could have done with a bit more cling film, so I used it sparingly and wrapped them the best way I could, then gently eased my boots back on and got myself down for breakfast.

Though my feet were far from perfect, the Vaseline was a great comfort to them. By rights, with the state of my feet the night before, I shouldn't have been able to stand up on them at all. Somehow regardless to what my body was saying, my brain was still making me do it.

After yesterday, today had to be a good day, surely things just couldn't get any worse but I can tell you by the time today was over I think I had reached one of the lowest points of the whole trip!

About 7am or just after, I walked out into the cool morning air. Usual thing was to set up the satnav and get a signal, well managed to get a signal alright this morning but things didn't quite get off to a good start. Instead of taking me back out on to the main road my satnav decided to lead me into the surrounding housing estate.

The estate was fairly new, in fact still under construction in parts and I was soon to run into navigational problems. Partly I guess because I haven't updated my satnav for years and before long it got me totally confused about which direction to head. I can only imagine it was trying to follow an old route which had now been altered.

I really couldn't afford to be taken on a wild goose chase, I had a long day ahead of me, 30 miles in fact. Almost in panic mood already I just had to find the right route and fast, walking out in the wrong direction would have been disastrous.

People were getting up and getting ready for work and school and I just had to catch someone on their way out of their house. I spotted a young girl by a car on her drive. I walked over and very politely asked if she knew which direction I needed to head to get to Frome.

She was of little use so I further asked if her parents could spare me a moment. Her mum came out but didn't have a clue either. All I could do now was to head back the way I'd come from. Frustrated that I was wasting valuable time, I spotted an old lady walking across the next junction

Optimistically I ask her if she could point me in the right direction to Frome. Well, she was as much use as a chocolate tea pot! She was a bit hard of hearing so I had to talk a bit louder and by the time she'd actually heard me, I think I was virtually shouting. All I was getting was:

"*Ay! Ay!*"

I could only laugh to myself when she finally replied to me in an excited high-pitched kind of voice expressing her disbelief that I could possibly be heading there.

"*Frome! Frome! That's miles away!*"

Yes, I thought, I know its miles away, 30 miles in fact, that's exactly why I don't want to be heading the wrong way!

So anyway, still not getting anywhere and the satnav still throwing a wobbler, third time lucky I spotted a fenced off part of the housing estate where just beyond these main gates were a few porta cabin type site huts.

I marched myself onto this site, half expecting to get stopped by somebody and straight up to the site huts and knocked the door. There was a young man inside who was at last of some help. He couldn't exactly tell me the way but at least was able to point me in the direction back to the main road.

At least from there I could pick up the route into Salisbury and then hopefully pick up the correct route on my satnav. When I finally reached the main road, I realised that I'd done full circle annoyingly almost back to where I'd started. Well at least now I was heading the right direction.

Followed the main road in towards Salisbury and fortunately very soon my satnav picked up a good route. As I headed towards town the traffic was building. Very soon the footpath I was following on my side of the road unfortunately came to an end and there right ahead of me were roadworks, a few hundred yards of coned off narrow lanes and no pedestrian access.

Pedestrians were now being diverted away from the road altogether. What was I going to do now I thought to myself, I'd already been messed about once today as it was. I simply had no choice in my mind other than to religiously follow the road regardless, I just wasn't prepared to take another risk. The traffic was now slow moving to queuing in places.

I proceeded forward expecting to get shouted at any moment by a member of the road working team or some angry driver passing by. I was tight against the cones with barely inches between myself and the traffic, surely my day couldn't get any worse I thought as the cones ended and were proceeded with a full height chain-link fence.

I was now literally pinned against a wire fence above my head with nowhere to escape whatsoever with buses and lorries passing within inches of me and my bag. I still remember thinking 'what the hell am I doing here? I must be mad!'

I had no choice but to keep on moving forward, out of the roadworks and out of harm's way. How I managed to escape abuse I really don't know, maybe it was just a really friendly area round here.

I barely touched the centre of Salisbury as my route took me back out away from the city centre and straight past the fire station. I stopped close by to there for a rest and a quick drink break. I was very soon back into the countryside. I think I was on the A360, what I do remember was it wasn't the widest of roads but it was very fast moving and I don't just mean cars.

There were some right dodgy spots along that road which made for some very dangerous walking. There were tall hedge rows close to the roads edge where the road would bear round tight bends with lorries thundering towards you at breakneck speed and my small bag was a lifesaving tool as I waved it out to alert oncoming drivers of my presence.

I mean it wasn't really an ideal situation but it sure gave me a few more inches breathing space as the traffic passed by. I still remember a very kind lady stopping and almost insisting I was to get in her car as she was so concerned for my safety on one section of that road that day.

As I said before, there were such kind people around; yet half an hour earlier, I had a lorry driver pass me on a straighter section of the road, tooting and swearing and waving his fingers at me because I hadn't crossed over to use a section of path that was only 20yards long. He was an aggressive driver with a foreign number plate might I add.

The last thing I needed was to add more unnecessary miles to my day even if it was just crossing the road and back. My feet today were far from comfortable but I had to keep pushing on, the storm yesterday had really taken its toll on them. I mean I admit they weren't in the best of states before the storm but with the water getting into my boots, it really hadn't helped as my skin softened up and peeled away.

I eventually got away from that dangerous section of road and right into some real countryside, turned off the A36 and onto a single-track country lane. Now this was more like it! Beautiful unspoilt countryside, no traffic, no noise, just open land.

This was the first section of proper country lane I'd walked since leaving London on Monday morning. I always knew it was going to be like this but to leave the main roads even for a brief period was like heaven. Unfortunately, it was relatively short lived.

After a few miles, I was back re-joining the main road, the A36. As I arrived at the junction there was a pub on the corner, there was a little garden down the side of it with some tables and benches just beckoning me in. Now I didn't want to be rude and just plant myself in somebody's garden but it was quite clearly a pub and I was desperate for a break, just a quick sit down, refuel and take the rucksack from my back and the weight off my feet.

Always such a relief to get it off your back even if just for a short while and surely, I wasn't doing any harm so I quietly entered and made myself at home. Of course, for all I knew I could have been entering the territory with some mad dog on the loose.

My feet were really beginning to suffer again. The cling film around my feet had started to perish and the Vaseline had started to dry out. It certainly seemed the right answer when I had started the day but the cling film displaced itself as I hobbled along, I realised I needed a lot more wrapping and a thicker layer of Vaseline if it were to be effective for a longer period of time to withstand the constant movement in my boots.

I set off from the pub at a slow past, gradually building up speed getting faster and faster as I eased my feet back into the pace. Every time I stopped now was a brief relief but only to struggle with the pain barrier every time I got going again.

Didn't get far up the road before I stopped at a small garage. As I said before, you never missed an opportunity to replenish supplies and while I was there, I also managed to pick up a new reel of cling film. If this film was going to help again, I needed to be plentiful with it.

I found a wall not far from the garage and spent some time working on my feet. I stripped off my boots and socks, re-wrapped them using the last of the Vaseline. My feet were still killing me from the damage from the storm on my way to Salisbury. The Vaseline was now an essential comfort and would hopefully see me all the way through to Frome.

What choice did I have? More worryingly, how was I going to get through tomorrow now the Vaseline was all but gone! There was a river running past nearby where I stopped. Bit of useless information I know but I remember a fisherman walking past me that day with his tackle in his hand, oops!

Doesn't sound a very appropriate way to put it, maybe tackle over his shoulder, mind not sure if that sounds much better either. Weird the sort of things you remember sometimes, things that stick in your mind.

One of the other things I picked up that day was a can of Red Bull energy drink. Never tried this stuff in my life before until now but feeling pretty tired out and thought I'd give it a go; I'd also been consuming the bits and pieces I'd brought with me day by day like energy bars and glucose tablets even.

Anyway, so I felt the need for a bit more of a boost and thought I'd check out this Red Bull. Well, I must say it didn't take long before I felt the effects from it, they really do work but the way young people take them on a daily basis or more, surely that can't be good for you.

Surely your system must get use to them and even start relying on them and then I can only imagine they become ill effective as a boost and more of essential requirement just to feel normal again! Then who am I to say? Personally, I think they're all crazy and there should be some kind of restriction regulating the sales of these products but that's just my opinion.

I soldiered on eventually making it to Warminster. I seemed to be consuming a lot more water than usual and by the time I was nearing Warminster my water supplies were getting dangerously low. The pain in my feet was gradually intensifying as I physically pushed them to their limits.

The greasy film around my feet had become too dry again and the film wrap was now rubbing against my skin and infuriating it more than ever. I needed to stop and get the film off but stopping at this point would have also been a painful task as getting going again would have been difficult.

My water situation was getting desperate almost to the point where I was getting tempted to knock on somebody's door and ask them to politely refill some of my bottles. I had learnt a lesson yesterday about having to consume more water but still wasn't carrying enough.

As I closed in on the town, I kept thinking surely there must be a shop around the next corner. The problem is when you get that tired your pace slows so much without you even realising and each mile seems further and further and seems to take forever. This walk was now beginning to really test me and my feet were on fire.

I needed to stop and relieve them and soon! They were in urgent need of some rest and recovery but right now that seemed so far away! My distance to Frome not actually that great but with the pace I was now achieving that seemed almost unreachable. I was trying to stay strong but the physical effect of my feet and legs was now having a detrimental effect on this.

I was finally saved dehydration by the promise of a garage ahead, I dragged myself there more than ready to collapse. I think I remember downing my rucksack outside before entering, left it lying by a pile of gas bottles and flowers, your usual old garage forecourt display. I replenished my supplies of water and food and yet another can of Red Bull.

After the kick I got out of one earlier, I thought another boost was more than welcome. I collapsed down outside the garage on a high kerb stone, a dirty old rotten petrol-stained dark hovel where I squeezed myself down but I was in no mood to be fussy.

It's hard to describe exactly how my feet were feeling at this point or indeed the way I was feeling. My feet were stinging in pain. Stopping seemed essential at this point but getting going again would be a real killer. I stripped my boots from my feet and cleared them of film.

I'd been reluctant to do this as I knew putting my socks and boots back on would be a painful task. I had no more Vaseline, so things weren't looking too good. I really was beginning to feel like this walk had got to the better of me. My mind wanted to carry on but my body was clearly telling me to stop, enough was enough!

Got chatting to a young lady on the forecourt, she was asking me what I was doing and wished me all the best with it. Despite the pain I was in, I didn't even mention to her how bad I felt, I was simply having a rest. How could I possibly stop now! How could I possibly not complete what I'd set out to do. I'd be a fraud, a failure, a liar, a cheat!

How could I face people again to say that I never done it! I was only four days into my walk and already contemplating failing. I had to deal with the situation now as it was. Firstly, I had to get to Frome, then I needed to consider where I went from there.

Like dangling a carrot on a stick in front of a donkey I was sitting there in this forecourt watching numerous taxis turn up the side road which ran alongside the garage. Against all wishes I was now coming round to the reality of hitching a lift to Frome, temptation getting closer and closer as I hauled myself to my feet.

At the speed I was now walking I'd have been lucky to have made it to Frome by midnight, plus the later I arrived the shorter recovery time my feet would have before setting off again tomorrow. I stumbled to my feet using my stick to help me keep balance and help shift some of the weight to my upper body.

Even the weight of my rucksack was getting to me and as I tried to stand up it was pulling me over. I had to stand up first and then reload my back. I then hobbled over to the roads edge keeping an eye out for an empty cab passing by.

Typically, now there were none to be seen. I waited around for a few minutes which felt like an age. Realising standing here was not helping I decide to move on to Warminster, keeping my eyes peeled on route. As I neared the town centre every step seemed a huge effort.

My mind was now set, along the high street ahead of me I could see the taxi rank. Hallelujah, I was saved. I needed a cash point and I couldn't believe it, not only was I in reach of both a taxi and a cash point but also there on the opposite side of the high street was Boots the Chemist. My golden opportunity for essential medical supplies.

I dragged myself across the road, luckily it wasn't much later in the day as the store was soon to be closed. As I shuffled my way across the shop floor I may as well have been walking on drawing pins or hot coals or even shards of glass, my feet were in so much pain!

I found the largest pot of Vaseline I could find in the store, can't say I've ever bought it before, I've heard it has its uses but I can assure you I've never been that way myself. Let's not get onto that subject as I don't want to offend anyone, mind I do get a bit sick of it rammed in your face on the TV every time you turn it on these days.

So, I went to the checkout then slowly and painfully made my way out of the shop, made my way to a cash point a few doors down and then crossed the road and over to the taxi rank.

My heart was sinking as I boarded a taxi. This seemed so wrong. I really felt like some kind of cheat or fraud but physically I had no choice in the matter. I even removed my charity bib as I felt so ashamed of what felt like failure. Even though I did not know anyone, it felt like I was being watched or judged, somebody was going to report back about me cheating my challenge.

The taxi driver didn't seem 100% sure of the way but I had my satnav set up already, plus of course it was a great way of making sure that he wasn't ripping me off and taking me a longer route. I wasn't that far from Frome but with the condition my feet were in, I had to accept defeat.

He dropped me off at the back of the Inn. It must have taken me a few minutes just to hobble through the carpark and round to the front door. I crashed into a chair in the reception, well I mean I didn't crash into it but I threw myself down as soon as I could as I couldn't wait to get the weight off my feet.

I ripped the boots off my feet as soon as I could, my feet were screaming out for freedom. I sat there for a while recomposing myself before dragging myself up to the reception desk. When I eventually arrived in my room, I crashed on my bed and threw my belongings down wherever I could, I now had blisters upon blisters thanks to yesterday's storm!

I thought I had a cunning trick up my sleeve. I had with me, a product my wife had bought called 'New Skin' or something like that. Unfortunately, what I thought was about to help me actually did the opposite. In my infinite wisdom I pealed back my flapping skin and sprayed this product directly onto my bare flesh, not of course anticipating what was about to happen next.

No instant reaction but count to about ten and there was nothing you could do; the damage was now done! As the chemicals started to do their work, my bare flesh suddenly felt like it was bubbling up on the surface, boiling away from the inside. I may just have well poured salt and vinegar into my bare wounds and stirred it round with a hot soldering iron.

Crippling pain shot through my foot in an instant, you know the pain when you just want to chop something off! Well, it was like that! Fortunately, the pain soon settled but I'd learnt my lesson and that happened to be the last time I used that stuff even to this day!

Still don't know whether I actually used that stuff correctly or not. To be quite honest I don't really self-medicate unless it seems essential, I only take tablets when I have to and would only use a plaster if my arm was falling off. I'm a great believer of self-healing being given a chance first.

Some of you tough ones may be thinking that I'm making a big fuss about nothing but I beg to differ. Personally, I think I have a high pain threshold and I rarely get ill. I'm usually the last one in my household to go down with anything when the viruses are making their rounds.

I'd now clocked up over 120miles since I'd left St Paul's Cathedral with 13 plus kilos on my back. I left home with a swollen left ankle, sore skin on my heels and what now sounds as though I had a broken toe on my right foot!

All of this as well as barely any relative proper training. All sounds a bit crazy when I put it like that. I knew this was going to be a test of my endurance but didn't quite expect it to be quite so harsh quite so soon!

I was shivering slightly; I think this was my body reacting to the pain. I had this last night after the dizzy spell I had. I run myself the deepest bath you could imagine. Of course, I had to go through the same old routine. Into a dry bath then gradually introduce cool water over my feet then gradually increase the temperature and depth until my bath was filled literally to the brim.

I even closed the overflow outlet with my feet to allow the water to reach full capacity of the bath. I had to lay still and laying back in the water after turning the taps off was a bit tricky. I think if I'd have farted the bath would have overflowed!

I didn't soak too long in the bath; I soon released the overflow and allow the water to slowly slip away then came the plug as I was glad to loss the water. I'm not really one for a deep hot bath usually, I can find it quite stifling sometimes. I'm much more of a tepid water kind of person, I just find it more refreshing.

I smothered my feet once again with Sudocrem to try to reduce the redness and help stop any infections, then down to dinner again in my socks and with the help of my stick. Although I can remember the Inn and its surrounds vividly, I can't seem to remember the layout of the restaurant at that one.

What I do remember mind was sitting there with my legs stretched out on the seat in front of me, I just needed my feet off the floor to give them maximum relief. Despite the fact of having such a devastating day I still couldn't contemplate the thought of having to give it all up.

Somehow, I don't know how but somehow, I was going to get up in the morning and just carry on regardless. Worryingly, I had another mega stretch again tomorrow, about 35miles again!

# Chapter 10
# The Bridal Way

Up early Friday morning. Every morning, I seemed to have more and more to do when I got up. Hay fever tablets, ibuprofen, bottles of water and generally repack sack as most of its contents would be spread across the room, my feet yet again too sore to sort things out the night before.

Got up early, half as optimistic as before knowing my feet were less than sufficiently recovered. Placed them down on the carpet, yes still a bit sore, surprise, surprise! Smothered them completely in a good thick layer of Vaseline, then wrapped them well, right up my legs past my ankles.

I must say it was a bit of a strange sensation walking around with my feet immersed the way they were but at least the pain was then more tolerable. I then put my socks and boots back on so as they had time to adjust while I sat and had breakfast.

Now I was in a bit of a dilemma this morning. It was still hugely playing on my mind that I'd cut my walk short yesterday and jumped in that damn cab. Now I know being realistic, I had no choice but it was still bugging me never the less.

Do I now get another cab and get the driver to drop me off where I got picked up yesterday or do I carry on walking from here? I really was in two minds. With the help of my phone and the internet, I'd done some calculations the night before, to check out the distances from where I'd got a lift. As it was, it turned out to be virtually the same distance from there to Yeovil as the distance from where I was now.

Logically then I would be walking the same distance. Of course, if I went back to where I was yesterday and walked via the Premier Inn I was at now, then sure it would be a few miles longer but it would seem ludicrous walking the wrong direction first, if you know what I mean.

If you don't get what I'm on about its quite simple really, when I booked, I didn't think I could make it from Salisbury to Yeovil so I booked Frome in between as a safer option which actually took me slightly off course and out of my way!

Anyway, I decided to take the logical option ad walk directly from where I was now at Frome. Even when I look back now, I would have been mad to have added unnecessary mileage, given the state of my feet. I just had to get on with it and get over it.

I set off straight after breakfast as early as I could as always. The Vaseline kind of squelching round my feet was a great relief I can tell ya! I remember having to stop a few times having to adjust the tightness of my laces.

Getting that right was so important, too tight and it would be crippling, cutting off the calculation and too much pressure around my feet and too loose and my boots would be flopping around as I walked along then causing more rubbing and more friction.

I soon arrived in Frome town centre itself. Nice little town, very hilly, seemed to pass hundreds of school kids as I passed through. Coming out of town was a real steep climb but it was early, I was at my fittest for the day so I just kept pushing upward.

Climbing gradients with sore feet I found a lot less painful than descending; you seem to have a lot more control when you're going up at where you place the weight on your feet. Had another long stretch again today, all 35miles of it.

Very soon got out into the countryside, which isn't hard round these parts, you don't have to walk far to find yourself out of the urban area and out into greener pastures. Yet again today as before I was offered a few lifts. I was still walking the main roads but all was a bit quieter today with a lot less traffic than previous routes.

Still, the road was fast and not always the best place to be on foot. I had a lady pass me and actually turn round and come back to see if I needed a lift. She was just so kind. She happened to be travelling the same direction as me, knew it was a fair old way to the next town and very kindly thought of helping me out.

Of course, I had no choice but to refuse. There was no way on this planet I was going to step foot in another vehicle after feeling so bad last night. I was probably being a bit harsh on myself, I don't mean not excepting a lift, I mean still beating myself up about doing a few miles in that cab last night.

I mean they were miles in the wrong direction and also thinking back I'd done a few extra miles when I got lost on the way between Staines and Egham, plus also walking round Basingstoke when I was in need of essential supplies!

That wasn't the only lift I was offered today. Further up between Wanstrow and Batcombe, I was offered a lift by another lady travelling the same way. She was parked in the layby opposite, she wound down her window. To my amazement she was about ninety years old. I'm not too sure who would have been taking the biggest risk, her or me!

Her at her age picking up some complete stranger, I mean that's risky enough at any age or me accepting a lift from somebody who probably couldn't see further than the bonnet! Anyway, so kind of her to offer. If I remember right, she gave me a donation for my charity.

I don't remember it being a large amount but some change from her purse and for all I know it may well have been her last few bob. I was very grateful to her and told her I must get on my way and passed her a few leaflets; I'd learnt from earlier on my walk to carry a few leaflets in my small bag.

Unfortunately, as I put the cash away and passed a leaflet to her, I managed to lose hold of my stick which was a real pain. Sore enough already, I had to struggle down to the floor, virtually laying down on my stomach with my rucksack on my back, desperately trying to reach my stick from under her car and praying she'd heard what I'd said to her and wasn't about to run me over.

That would have been ironic, I could see the headlines now, '*Old lady stops to help charity walker and ends up running him over!*'

I bit further on and I was stopped by a lorry driver looking for some farm to deliver to. Amazing isn't it that I'd just spoken to more people in these last few miles than anywhere else on my walk. It really does seem in general that the further you get away from London, the more friendly people become. Amazingly if I remember rightly, it wasn't until I'd got past Bagshot till, I got the first 'good morning' from somebody.

A bit further up and my satnav lead me on a route that I wasn't expecting. At Pitcombe it led me right off the main road and out into the countryside onto an old bridal way. Up until now it had been main roads all the way. Even yesterday when it led me through a little village, I still never left the tarmac, so I wasn't expecting this at all.

As I veered off from the main road, I was led down a dark dingy, tree lined, very narrow lane. 'Pitcombe' the sign said, well it certainly felt like I was heading down into a pit. As it bottomed out and lead out from the trees I was led through or under you could say, an old railway arch type structure with a few houses dotted around.

Beyond this the tarmac soon ended as the narrow lane transformed into a mud track. It was a fair steep gradient now and not so flat and comfortable under foot. When I look back now it was saving me a short deviation in the main road and only to be joining it further on, at the cost of a very steep hill and much rougher terrain.

I now had to navigate myself across tufts of grass, deep tyre tracks from the local tractors and troughs of water from the recent rain. You also seem to lose all control of how you place your feet down on ground like this.

My stick was now vital at keeping me from stumbling and testing the depth of any unavoidable puddles as I knew how devastating it could be if I were to get water in my boots again. Avoiding the rocks and odd boulder and of course the odd dogs deposit was all a bit of a game I could of done without.

Of course, not all dog deposits are left on the ground, some very kind dog owners seem to like to bag them up and hang them on nearby trees and fence posts for decoration nowadays! Aren't they just charming!

I still remember my back getting sweatier and sweatier as the load on my back began to feel heavier and heavier as I climbed the hill with the sun beating down on me. The clouds in the distance were gathering once again, they had been for a while now! I could hear the rumbling of thunder once again in all different directions. It seemed almost inevitable I would be battling the elements once more.

I must admit I did feel a little bit vulnerable and lonely out in the middle of nowhere, all on my tod and way away from the nearest main road or any passing traffic. A sprained ankle or a fall here would be the last thing I needed and the thought did go through my mind you could be laying there for days before somebody came by to help you.

Of course, I had my phone on me but this is the typical place where your phone doesn't work due to lack of reception. The path proceeded up through a thick tree lined area which did seem a bit eerie on my own and the ground here was all that bit softer and wetter where the sun couldn't quite shine through to dry it out.

As it opened out on to the summit to a much wider path and more open land, I could see in the distance a tractor and an open backed truck and a few workmen. As I neared the first chap, he spoke in a friendly way just passing the time of day. Can't remember the exact conversation now but it was something to do with me passing this way. I'm guessing it wasn't a very well used path by strangers.

What I do remember clearly was his surprised look on his face when I told him I was walking to Land's End, he seemed quite amazed. As I was walking away and his mates came over to him, I heard him exclaim.

*"That man's walking all the way to Land's End!"*

He said it as if I was crazy!

The storm clouds were continuing to gather and the thunder getting louder and more frequent. I soon made it to the end of the track and was back on the main road. I was beginning to feel real tired and my feet real sore again. The lumps and bumps had not helped to say the least.

I made it to a service station in desperate need of a break, don't get me wrong, I'd stopped several times already today but some places stood out more than others. I couldn't wait to sit down and take the weight off my legs for a minute.

My calves were aching again and I was getting to the stage again where I was having to spray my legs periodically with deep heat to keep them at ease. I sat and downed another can of Red Bull as I still had a fair way to go and was feeling a bit wore out, mind after yesterday's performance I was amazed I was still going!

I stripped the boots from my feet and reapplied some more Vaseline and rewrapped them. If anyone would have seen me doing it, they would have thought I was mad. The continuous pounding over the miles I had covered and of course the bumpy bridal track hadn't helped as the cling film had moved around and become very uncomfortable.

The storm was now virtually overhead with much more lightening as well. The rain was now inevitable so once again I prepared for the worse. As I rose to my feet once again, I had to rely on my stick to stop me stumbling. My pace again was slow to begin with till I gradually pushed myself harder and harder and got back up to a good rhythm.

Every time I stopped my legs seemed to just seize up working. I knew today was going to be a tough one and I'm not sure sometimes if knowing how far you had left to walk was a help or a hindrance. Sometimes the miles seemed to pass so slowly.

As I neared towards Yeovil, I passed through a small settlement called Queens Camel, pretty little village with a quaint church. I had to laugh as I came into the village as I passed a sign warning the approaching traffic of traffic calming ahead.

There in the distance was a parked car, not illegally parked but all the same causing chaos as the evening rush began to build. It was like one of those silly signs you see at the seaside or on a silly micky take TV show.

Out through the village and the heavens began to open, rain was teaming down once again, pouring down my face, stinging my eye from the insect repellent once again on my head. As I came away from the village once again the footpaths seized to exist and I was forced back to road walking.

Given the rush hour was now under full swing and the poor visibility, walking the kerb side with huge lorries ploughing towards me wasn't for the faint hearted. Biggest and by far the most dangerous risk came from vehicles rammed up the backside of other vehicles, drivers that don't care for allowing any distance between them and the vehicle in front regardless to weather conditions.

Using my small green bag, I could wave it around and alert most oncoming traffic of my presence but trying to get the attention of drivers travelling too closely behind was not quite so easy!

Fortunately for me today the water runoff was nothing compared to that I'd experienced on the A30 yesterday where it was running down the hills with nowhere to go. The rain calmed as the storm passed over and gradually moved away.

As I neared towards Yeovil town centre, my legs and feet had just about had enough and I couldn't wait to reach my destination. I was stopping more and more frequently as the day wore on and seemed to be consuming more and more fluids.

As I closed in on the town centre my satnav took me away from the main road and directly through the middle of a housing state. I desperately needed one last stop, a quick drink and a bite, another protein bar or a snicker or whatever I had handy in my small bag.

Unfortunately, you just don't seem to get many seats on a housing estate and I didn't want to just plonk myself down on somebody's garden wall for the fear of upsetting someone. I'm sure they probably wouldn't have been over fussed but I didn't want to be rude.

In one of the gardens directly ahead of me I spotted a gentleman washing his car on his drive way. Surely, he wouldn't mind if I perched on his wall for a few ticks, I mean what harm would I be doing? I spoke, said hello and just ask him.

He didn't hesitate to be accommodating, maybe just out of politeness but that was as far as the conversation went. He really didn't have any intention of carrying on any real kind of conversation at all. Maybe he was a bit unsure of me, after all I don't suppose it's every day you get a complete stranger hiking past your house loaded down like I was and right in the middle of a housing estate.

More logical perhaps to see someone walking down the main roads or country lanes but of course with the use of these satnavs nowadays it's just a case of taking the shortest distance and right past his house happened to be my route.

Seemed at little bit strange to me that he was washing his car given the weather conditions, ok it had stopped lashing it down but the thunder was still rumbling around in the distance.

When I finally reached the Premier Inn, I was so relieved. It was almost like finding an oasis in a desert. Satnavs are such fantastic tools and, in my experience, I have found them so reliable. Without the use of a satnav, I don't think I could ever have managed to cover the ground I was covering because of the extra time you would need to navigate and of course the risk of making a mistake could have had dire consequences.

Once again that evening, I was down in the restaurant in my socks and my stick to support me. With my feet still extremely sore, I requested a table not too far away. There was a young man there at the next table sitting there with his girlfriend, he kept trying to sort of wink at me. I think he was just being friendly and don't even go where, what I mean is I think he had overheard the conversation I'd had with the waiter 'about my walk' and he was just trying to befriend us.

Unsure of his intentions, mind I was a bit cautious with the eye contact which is hard when you're sitting so close and you can feel someone sitting there smiling at you, if he had something to say then just say it. Mind can't say I was really in the mood for conversation, I had my feet up on the bench and all I wanted to do was grab some food and get back up to my room and rest up for another long day tomorrow.

I do remember having to complain about my drink. I ordered a Pepsi with no ice. Well, it wasn't the fact that it came with ice that annoyed me so much, it was more to do with the fact that it tasted like some kind of watered-down soda stream. Even without the ice it didn't really taste brilliant but it was certainly an improvement. I don't really complain much to be honest, well only when it's justifiable.

I don't think enough people complain enough in this country and that's why service can sometimes get so slack in some places. If I do complain it's not about getting money off but more to the fact if nobody complains they'll just go on delivering up the same old crap in the same old way and think it's acceptable.

My wife's more likely to complain than I am, largely I'd say because she's a bit more particular than I am with her food. I remember once sitting in a restaurant and the waitress coming over to ask if everything was ok with her food and my wife answered her with:

*"No not really!"* and followed it with about six or seven complaints! The poor waitress didn't know what had hit her! I did feel a bit sorry for her that day, mind it's only because so few people complain about the crap food and service that it ends up becoming the norm in some places.

I did once get so fed up waiting for bill in one place that I said to the passing waiter:

*" Could I possibly have the bill before my credit card expires!"* followed by a sharp kick from my wife, which was rich coming from her; which also reminds me of once years ago when she kept kicking me under the table. We were sitting in a vicar's office being interviewed to be married and I kept saying 'oh god!' and 'Jesus Christ!'

Not thinking what I was saying, mind in this modern world things like that must happen all the time don't they or is it just me!

I shan't go on about this much more but I do also remember being in a restaurant once and after one person complained, the next minute the whole restaurant was complaining about the same thing, it was almost like a comedy and in a b & b once we complained about the tea as it was so bad, sent it back and ordered the coffee.

Next minute everybody was copying us. I think they were using some kind of economy, economy teabags, hung out to dry from last week or the week before. You never forget those moments.

Anyway, so back to this evening. Finished my food then back up to my room. I must admit although my feet were sore, they weren't as bad as they'd been the evening before and I had a bit of a break to look forward to tomorrow, only 32.5 miles to go!

This was my last evening on my own. My mate Edd would be joining me the following evening, which was something to look forward to. Only problem was going to be I'd have to keep my room a damn site tidier than I had up until now and keep my gear in better order somehow.

# Chapter 11
# No Cream Teas Today!

Saturday 18<sup>th</sup> June. Up early again this morning but not quite as early as usual, breakfast slightly later this morning, not through choice but because it was Saturday morning. Breakfast is served later at the weekend as you don't get the business people staying so I had a bit of a lay in.

Destination today, Honiton. Wanted to stay on track today as I was meeting my mate this evening, he was travelling down by train to meet up with us.

Feet didn't feel too bad today, in fact it was probably the best they had felt for a few days which was a bit of a relief, seemed to be on the mend slightly or at least coping with the pain. I couldn't honestly see them improving that much as they still had a fair punishment ahead of them.

Today would see me cross the half way point which was great but of course you have to be realistic and take on board that I was starting the second half with my feet in somewhat worse condition than I started the first.

Before I did anything at the start of the day, I had one very important issue to sort out. I don't remember now the precise issue but it was something to do with an issue over the address of the Honiton Inn. I think the google address or postcode to be more specific was in disagreement with the post code on my paperwork.

My distance today was slightly less than the previous few days but I can assure you after walking another 32.5 miles I was not going to be in the mood to be walking around Honiton aimlessly not knowing where the Premier Inn was located. I got down slightly earlier than I needed and raised the issue with the lady at reception.

She fully understood my concerns and I must admit she was fantastic, she looked it up for me and even printed off a map of the final location. The staff were all great there, even had a bacon sandwich made up for us for on the road.

As I said I had a great day today. I don't know if it was because I had something to look forward to or what but it really did go well and I even remember enjoying parts of the walk. I'm not saying I hadn't enjoyed it so far, it's more that the pain had smothered the enjoyment most of the time.

I'm guessing the fact I was meeting up with my mate this evening and the fact I would be finishing today with more miles behind me than in front, were two big contributing factors lifting my spirit.

I set off from Yeovil at a reasonable time, not quite as early as usual, being weekend but still early. I set off at a good pace heading once again for the A30. Me and that A30 had become quite close on this trip, a bit too close at times I can tell Ya and today was going to be no exception.

The walk out from Yeovil town centre out towards the A30 was mainly uphill. I enjoyed the fresh morning air and the lack of motorist clogging up the roads. Saturday morning did have its advantages.

Again, today was no walk in the park but I felt in the right mood to just push myself that little bit harder. The pain in my feet definitely felt easier today, my legs felt fine, my back felt good and I was ready to take on the world, bring it on!

As I said, the A30 wasn't so kind to me today. To be honest, in places it was a bit tricky, a bit dangerous in places and extremely dangerous in others. Our roads in Britain are not geared up for walkers at all. In places they felt a bit more like suicide alley.

Anyway, I did survive, else I wouldn't be sitting here now writing this. Losing a foot path is one thing but losing a foot path and a verge on an extremely fast road with ten foot plus hedges alongside with twists and bends and crazy drivers is not so much fun. I certainly did a lot more road walking today than I would have liked but there wasn't a whole lot I could have done to resolve that.

I suppose I could have stayed in Yeovil, wrote to every council along the A30 between Yeovil and Honiton, expressing my concerns for more footpaths and hedge trimming but by the time anything would have been done I'd have been old and grey and my family would have forgotten who I was and where I was and what I was doing and that would have been just waiting for a reply!

Passed through a few villages which was great as this was usually your best chance of finding a seat for a quick break along the way. Past through West Cocker and on to East Chinnock. There's a part of the A30 just before you get into East Chinnock that I found most fascinating.

As the A30 winds down from the east side the road cuts through a small strip of woodland. Either side of the road there I was amazed to find almost vertical embankments with the land held back with what appeared to be partly synthetic and partly natural.

The steep sides appeared to be a combination of some kind of cement-based mortar mix with tree roots wrangling their way in and out, weaving themselves down the wall like surface of the retaining slopes.

There were parts there with full trees growing out of the top edges of these embankments, appearing as if like magic with nothing beneath them for support as their branches stretch out wide across the road beneath. I took one photo on my phone but have since also looked them up on the internet and still find them fascinating.

I must admit I did set out with intentions of taking many more pictures than I actually did but unfortunately due to the pain I'd been in so much of the time, stopping was often the last thing I wanted to do unless it was for a necessary drink break or for food etc.

Every time I stopped it was almost certain pain to get going again but as I said I felt a bit more comfortable today so I took the opportunity to take a few snaps.

I did pass through a bigger settlement, the town of Crewkerne. It seemed the obvious place for a proper rest and a food break. As I drew into the town, I found myself a lovely bench to park myself right outside The George Hotel.

If you're wondering how I can remember all these details like place names and pubs and things, well I don't, the truth is since I've been back, I've retraced some of my steps on the internet and been able to get further information from there. It seems strange now when I look back and zoom in on some of the places I was sitting or taking a break, it very quickly brings back memories.

As I said I wasn't really in the mood for taking photographs most of the time and I certainly wasn't in the mood for taking notes, besides at this stage I hadn't even thought about writing a book but funny enough it was this day that I did have the idea.

So, I sat outside The George Hotel, right in the centre of town, opposite the town hall. I was very much enjoying the break until I had the sudden urge to move on. This time it wasn't my schedule that prompted me. Now I know a few of you are going to hate me for saying this or maybe a lot of you, so I'll apologise now but you have to remember that this is my own opinion, which surely, I'm entitled to. Morris dancers, Morris dancers, Morris dancers!

Sorry but I just don't get it! Grown men prancing around with bells attached to their ankles, dancing with ribbons, historic as it may be but embarrassment of the country if you ask me. I know people are going to hate me for saying it but when you look at the wonderful ways some other nations resemble their history or way of life, Morrie dancers, really! Nah!

Anyway, so time to move on, back on to the crazy A30. I'm sure this day was the day I came within inches of catching a lift by a bus involuntarily. I think I was lucky to have survived when I literally had to dive into a hedge to miss being taken out by some mad coach driver. It was also the day I nearly lost my stick, now that would have been a disaster.

Didn't leave it behind in a shop this time, no I accidently placed the end of it down and unluckily caught the slotted gap in a wrought iron drain cover. The tip lunged down between the gaps by only a mere few inches but as it did so and as I proceeded forward the narrow gap restricted the movement on my stick, snatched it completely out of my hand and it rebounded and stopped back upright behind me.

It all happened so quickly within the blink of an eye, as I turned back on myself and tried to grab the top end of it, it was almost like watching a disaster unfolding in slow motion that you are unable to prevent. As I missed the top of the stick it had begun to make its decent down into the deep dark depths below the road surface, my heart sank as I watched it disappear in front of me.

I was snatching at it as it dropped, sinking into the ground, then it abruptly came to rest barely an inch protruding. Phew! That was close! I had really became quite attached to my stick and at times it really did play a vital role in steadying me along the way as well as heaving me up the steep gradients and easing me down the slopes.

That wasn't the only accident I had with my stick. Thinking back again I think it was the day I walked to Frome, I dropped my stick out of my hand and in an attempt to save it from completely descending to the ground I sort of caught the top edge of it with my right leg.

Well, this sort of did the trick but as I proceeded forward, naturally the bottom end of the stick lodged itself somehow onto the tarmac and in the process the top end nearly took out my soft parts on its way up. Just the thought was enough to bring tears to my eyes.

The problem is you get tired and complacent and gradually loosen your grip as you plod along, till you have a reminder like this of how your most treasured aid can suddenly become a lethal weapon against you!

I passed through another small settlement called Chard and shortly after this and not a second too soon, my satnav led me away, right away, from the busy crazy main road. It was like entering a different world. At last, I was well away from that noisy, hellhole rat race of a highway.

Playing chicken with the waves on a sandy beach trying not to get your shoes wet is one thing but playing chicken on the tarmac with speedy motorist and huge juggernaut's thundering towards you, where your life is at stake, is a peril I could happily do without.

Now, I was actually beginning to enjoy myself, leisurely strolling the long narrow country lanes edged with low hedgerows and beyond that fields and hills rolling all the way to the horizon. Plentiful sightings of nature in progress with beautiful butterflies fluttering by, birds in the trees and bees busy pollinating the wild flowers amongst the hedgerows.

You could also hear the sound of the crickets and grass hopers in the long grasses. Peace at last bar the joyful sound of nature in its abundance. I did see a huge amount of amazing butter flies on the course of my walk which reminds me, why are butter flies called butter flies?

I've always thought they should be renamed flutter byes as that exactly what they do. No doubt there's some scientific reason how they got their name. And why we're on the subject I've always called a squirrel a sqwizzel, I just like the sound of it. Don't worry, my children probably think I'm mad too!

Walking these narrow country lanes, I felt so much more relaxed. I was passing the time away singing to myself out loud, can't honestly remember now what I was singing, just whatever tune had to be ringing in my head at the time.

For the first time for a few days, I was really thinking of my family at home and what they were up to. It's not that I hadn't been thinking of them at all up until now but more for the reason my mind was so consumed with the effort I was having to put in and the pain I'd been going through at times.

I had spoken to my wife and the boys every day and yes, I was missing them all. I've never been away from the family before so it was all a bit strange for us and I can only imagine it must have been a bit strange for them too, me not being at home.

As I walked the glorious green pastures of the countryside the silence was only broken on the odd occasion by the clattering sound of a tractor and trailer pulling its load up and down the lanes. The same old tractor appeared time and time again, big green one with matching trailer, virtually taking up the whole width of the lane as it passed by.

The driver was either blind or just dam ignorant as he passed by with barely an inch between us. The huge big rubbery tyres past within inches of my toes and the air behind him a bit unsavoury from his load in the breeze.

Only disadvantage of these lanes was finding somewhere to park your backside for a rest can be quite challenging at times. I found myself a bit of a slope on a patch of ground at the edge of a junction where it was not too overgrown. I would always try to avoid completely flat land as it was a chore getting back up again.

I must admit although not perfect, this was the best my feet had been for a few days. While I was at this junction an elderly gentleman pulled up alongside accompanied by two ladies in the back of his car. He drew alongside and lowered his window to see if I was ok or needed a lift at all.

Very, very nice of him, I did meet some real lovely people on my walk. Had a bit of a chat with the two ladies in the back and both of them donated a small sum of money from their purses which was really kind of them!

Further on from here my walk took me straight through a little village, Stockland if I recall correctly. Quaint little village I do recall with well-trimmed hedges, beautifully kept gardens and well-kept houses. Bumped into one of the locals as I passed through, charming man, proud of his small community, he was telling me how the local village pub had recently closed down and how devastating this was to this little community.

He seemed quite upset about it. I do hope they managed to save it somehow. It seems to be the theme of late with pubs closing up all over the country but in such communities like that it can be quite devastating to the residents, particularly the older generations.

It was great now and again having a chat with people, helped break up the boredom of being on your own, mind most of the time up until now I wasn't in the best of moods for chatting.

I was bang on target today for reaching Honiton at reasonable time. Aiming to arrive at about 6:30pm if I remember right. It was sweltering hot that afternoon and I remember having to strip off a bit as you get pretty warm with that rucksack strapped on for hours.

It had been pretty hilly today, mind despite this I seemed to make excellent time, strangely enough I found it easier walking up hill than anything else. I admit it zapped more energy but it just seemed easier on my feet.

Somehow it allowed you to choose where to put the pressure on your feet but the down side of this for every hill you climbed naturally you must come down the same distance. This was not always quite so forgiving.

A few miles further on and yet again I was in desperate need of a break but just couldn't find anywhere to sit. Long grasses aren't always a great option, as you really needed some kind of proper visual on what you were about to sit on, I'd already sat right down in the middle of an ant's nest once, I think it was on my way to Basingstoke or Salisbury.

I eventually found a patch of mowed lawn alongside a farmer's gate. I pulled the weight from my back and crashed down for a moment. Over the fence I could see huge plastic greenhouse like structures stretching for quite a distance down towards some old farm house. Obviously, a working farm growing some kind of fruit or vegetables or both.

The grass wasn't really ideal, a bit flat for my liking, so a bit awkward for getting up again. The road here was fairly narrow with hedges on both side so I was careful not to protrude my feet too far out for the fear of some vehicle racing round the bend and taking my feet with them on their way past or worst still seeing my feet at last minute and swerving straight towards me.

The lawn was neatly mowed on one side and from the other side I could see this long narrow strip appeared to lead down to what I was guessing was the farm entrance in the distance. I could just make out some kind of black board with some kind of signage on it. My eyes are pretty good at long distance but this was a bit too far!

Couldn't stop for too long as I really wanted to keep on schedule today so I was soon back on my feet, loaded up strapped up and set off again. As I soon neared the entrance to the farm, I just couldn't believe my eyes, I could not believe it! It was like having a real-life Victor Meldrew occasion, I just could not believe what I was reading.

Yes, it was the entrance to the farm but the sign was not a sign for delivery drivers, tractors or the postman, neither was it advertising any kind of produce nor pick your own strawberry's or anything like that. Hung on a white metal frame was a black swing board with big white letters across it and read 'OPEN for award winning cream teas and morning coffees.

I could have killed for a cup of tea, any tea, let alone award-winning cream teas. Not just that but to tease me even more, sitting just beyond the neatly trimmed hedges was a proper table and chairs sitting in a beautifully kept English country garden. It was like a dream come true.

I had to pinch myself to check it was all real. I'm in the middle of nowhere down a tiny country lane out in the sticks and the last thing you would ever expect to find and there it was about 200yards from where I'd stopped.

117

What was the chance of that? I still laugh about it now. I really couldn't stop again as tempted as I was. Had a quick chat with the lady running it on my way past, I would have even got a service with a smile and it's not everywhere these days you can get that!

I guess there was a bit of irony there both ways, I mean I can't imagine they get that much business located where they are and there was me just yards away but clueless of what lie ahead. I would have happily have paid them double or more for a proper cup of tea and a proper sit down.

On I marched towards Honiton. Only thing I passed between here and the town was a few old cows in the field and a few sheep. Actually, they were nice cows, I even stopped at one and took a picture. They came right over to the metal frame gate to see me.

Tell a lie, I did pass one person on the way down towards Honiton, it was that lovely lady from the tea garden as she came cycling past me on her bike. She'd packed up for the day I guess and was on her way home. She recognised me from earlier and acknowledged me on her way past.

The road fell sharply as I dropped down towards the town centre, winding down and right under a railway bridge before opening out into the road below. Leading me up through the high street, following my satnav I was counting down the miles as I closed in on my destination.

I remember the high street distinctively with its old fashion water drainage system where the rain water drains down along the centre of the path with shaped concrete gutters instead off the kerbs as it usually does now.

I reached the Inn in plenty of time, managed to arrive ahead of my mate Edd. This must have been one of my best days I'd had so far physically. I'd clocked up a fair few mile today that was on top of the 153 miles I'd already done this week but physically today I was on top form.

What had really crippled my feet on top of all the existing problems was that storm I went through on Wednesday and I think the soreness on my feet had slowly improved since, mind I was still left with the consequential blisters which seemed to be a direct result from that.

I think the rest of my body had physically gained strength in some ways, like my back and legs, neck and shoulders. I'd been through that initial working my parts too hard syndrome but now they were toughening up and ready to take on more.

So, I arrived at the Premier Inn and for the first time I didn't literally crash in to the awaiting chair in the reception room. I did sit down and take the weight off my feet and again couldn't wait to get my boots off but I was in nowhere near the amount of discomfort I had previously been in. The staff at the Honiton branch were fantastic.

We had a quick chat and they were so friendly and accommodating. They even fetched me a pint of ice-cold water from the bar. They couldn't do enough for me. It was an unusual layout there I do recall, an open reception and bar, restaurant area. It was very friendly and before long I was also chatting to a few others sitting relaxing in the bar.

Checked in, got up to my room and bathed and changed before Edd arrived. Seemed real strange knowing I was going to have to share my room this evening, of course I couldn't throw my gear around like I had done up until now. I had to keep my room tidy and be more organised with my kit.

Strangest thing was sharing my room with another man, can't remember the last time that ever happened. Fortunately, we've been great mates over the years so all should be well. Other than the fact of sharing my room I was half looking forward to the company, not saying I hadn't enjoyed the last six days on my own.

Time on one's own can be nice sometimes, time to reflect and time to think about things properly. Self-analyse your life, think about your loved ones and where you'd like to be and things. Life can be a funny old thing sometimes, so predictable form day to day yet also so unpredictable.

Lots of people take paths in their lives that they never set out to do and so often life can change at the drop of a hat. Different paths we go down, often by luck or chance, sometimes good, sometimes not so good. Regardless to how you got to where you are in life you can't undo the past or change history but can make the most of what you do have and the future is always still unwritten.

I'd say the biggest asset I have always had in my mind is always being optimistic about whatever situation you're in. pessimism is a self-destructing attitude just like depression feeds off depression. The other thing I have learnt over the years is to be happy as you can regardless of your situation

I don't mean you have to be 100% satisfied with everything all the time that's not what I'm saying and it's healthy to have dreams and goals to work to but what I can say that if you go through life thinking if only, I had this, if only I had that, then you'll never be happy.

In my experience most people in life like that are never happy because they are always looking for a bit more and a bit more, always searching for the next more expensive buzz. Just remember as well, there's always some on else in life worse off than you.

Whoops! Starting to drift away again. What I was going to get on to was it was when I was walking through the countryside today that I first had thoughts about writing a book about this whole walk I was on.

So much seemed to have happened over the last few days like getting lost, going through the storm, barely being able to walk, meeting nice people, some not so nice, dodging the traffic, plus all the emotions I'd been through like the pain and being away from the family and I was only half way through.

So many memories in my head in such a short space of time. I was starting to think about all the months of planning and setting up stalls, planning my journey and being in the newspapers and on the radio show, etc.

A bit like when I decided to do this walk it all sort of happened in my mind so quickly. One moment I was thinking what it would be like to sit and write a book, the next moment or by the end of the day, should I say, I'd virtually convinced myself that I would be doing it!

Had to get back down to reception as Edd was due soon and for the first time, I had no phone reception in my room. Sat downstairs just inside the restaurant and with the bar in front of me as tempting as it was you may think, I sat there with my pint of lemonade or Pepsi enjoying my last few minutes of my own company.

Edd turned up all fit and well and certainly looked a bit fitter than I was feeling. It was great to catch up with him again, one of those friends, known him most of my life and we could go a year without seeing each other yet it felt like you could pick up the conversation like we were in the same room yesterday.

He'd got the train down and walked from the station. He had a fair load on his back, turned out to be mainly food unlike myself with about two weeks supply of clothes and essentials. Got himself checked in, took his gear up to the room then we got ourselves back down to the restaurant for dinner.

I must admit one of the strangest things to me so far had been sitting in a restaurant every night on my Jack Jones like some kind of billy no mates.

Seemed a bit surreal sitting in the restaurant with him, so many miles from home, pint in his hand, Pepsi in mine, I'd made a promise to myself not to have a single pint until I'd reached Land's End and I was sticking to it. It almost felt like some kind of real lads' adventure trip. Hadn't done anything like this for years, some thirty odd years to be exact.

As young lads we set off for the day on the train all the way up to the Lake District and back. British Rail were doing some special deal at the time if you had a student card, so we travelled to Windermere and back for next to nothing. Had a great day, never forgot it, don't think I'm going to forget this trip either.

After dinner I had to return downstairs one more time. Having no reception in my room I had to go out the front of the building to call my wife and boys like I did every night. What I wasn't expecting however was to receive another donation on the way back up.

Got chatting to some ladies in the lift on my way back up and one of them gave me a ten-pound donation from her purse. What a great end to the day!

# Chapter 12
# The Frustration!

Sunday 12th June.185 miles down, 150 to go! So, I'm well past half way. Up as early as we could be again, bearing in mind weekend breakfast hours. Sorted gear out as usual, tablets, foot wrap, water bottles, etc... breakfast and out. They were great staff at Honiton, enjoyed my stay but time to move on. Little bit of a break today, only 29 miles to go.

There was a garage directly next door so the first stop was to top up supplies. Thought I'd hand the satnav over to Edd, keep him occupied on the way plus give myself a break at the same time. Less time spent worrying about the route hopefully meant more time to concentrate on getting through the tedious and tiring pace of walking, walking and more walking.

Sometimes in life it's nice to be able to mentally relax, like doing a mundane job sometimes can be quite nice, mind I couldn't do it all the time but once in a while it's great to relax and just think of different things or even just nothing if that's possible. I guess it must be, some people seem to manage ok!

So anyway, now Edd had the controls, he also had a few maps tucked away in his rucksack and a phone to hand with a route to follow as well. How could we ever possibly get lost? Believe it or not as it goes, we nearly set off on the wrong foot. First stretch today was back down onto the dreaded A30.

Following the satnav even though set on walking route, we almost made the wrong move. Fair enough the satnav looks for the shortest route which is great but what it doesn't take into consideration is that when travelling on foot, you need to make sure you're on the right side of the carriageway, well when I say the right side, I don't mean not the wrong side, I mean not the left side.

Well, I do mean not the wrong side because the left side is the wrong side if you get what I mean. Anyway, so all ok on a normal road but when you're walking along a dual carriageway there's not always a safe place to cross over.

Experience has taught me you may well have a path or somewhere to walk when you join the carriageway but more often than not this will disappear a few miles up the road if not before. You may even find trees and shrubs that have grown out to the edge by the kerb, forcing you into the carriageway itself and walking the carriageway with the traffic behind you is really not where you want to be!

This was Edd's first stretch with me as we walked the edge of the A30. Of course, he did what any sane person would do and walked along the grass verge where possible, as far away from the roads edge as he could. Well, that's all ok had your feet not been in the condition mine were in and just done 180 miles from London.

Anything but perfect flat ground under foot to me was just pure torture. Luckily as it goes for most of the stretch, we done there was a very generous strip of tarmac between the painted white line of the carriageway and the grass verge. To Edd this was still far too close for comfort but if he had walked some of the stretches, I'd walked so far, I think he would have shared a different view.

Some of the stretches I'd been forced to walk on the single carriage main roads were like hell highways compared to this. I really don't think there would have been a cat in hells chance he would have set foot on them. I guess he would have turned back and found an alternative route somehow.

Wasn't too long before we were off the main carriageway and led on to a much quieter route. To be honest with you I'd prepared myself to do great big stretches following the main drag down so when it turned out that the satnav was to lead us off the main roads and onto smaller roads alongside wherever possible, this was a great bonus to me.

I was in Great Spirit to start with today and I must admit it seemed a bit strange to have a walking partner. One thing we would sort of have to get use to was who was leading who. There were going to be times when I needed to be up front as I was the one setting the pace as he was still really fresh but problem was with Edd now having control of the directions, he needed to be leading me.

Then there'd be times where I needed to be in front for safety purposes as I was much more visible to any oncoming traffic with my brightly coloured 'Make a Wish' bib and my small bright green bag that I had become a dab hand at using to maximised effect.

It was a much more enjoyable walk away from the speeding traffic on the main roads. You could sort of drop your guard a bit, still remain cautious of the occasional vehicle speeding past but it was largely now clear from the bulk of the traffic. Had to stop at one point and sort my laces out on my boots.

They were far too loose and my boots were moving around far too much on my feet. I still had the Vaseline on my feet but it was critical to get the laces to just the right tension. Too loose and too much movement, too tight and they'd be strangling my ankles.

Again, finding somewhere to sit was never easy and crouching down to the kerb side wasn't ideal either. Fortunately, I spotted a layby ahead with some heavy road working plant sitting dormant. They weren't exactly fenced off or any cones around them and surely, they wouldn't mind if I just climbed aboard one of them just to use the seat and sit comfortably while I sorted out my laces.

There was a huge bulldozer like digger at the front of the layby so I heaved myself up and into the driving seat to sort things out. Edd decided to take a few pictures. I remember laughing with Edd about taking a whole load of different pictures on the way down with me sitting on different vehicles as we made our way across the countryside, making out we'd done a bit of cheeky cheating here and there.

Towards lunchtime we neared the M5. I remember passing a big police headquarters as well somewhere along near there and realising I was in Devon. I'd crossed the border yesterday on the way to Honiton but not realising as I walked the small country lanes.

Reaching the M5 also seemed another great milestone, a bit like clearing the M25 felt like leaving London behind me, passing beneath the M5 felt like entering The West Country.

As we wandered in towards Exeter city centre, we both kept our eyes peeled for somewhere to sit down for lunch. We weren't cutting directly through the city centre but there was bound to be a seat somewhere along route. We did eventually find a seat, a great seat, smack bang on the centre of a grass verge with the most spectacular view you could ever wish for, a lovely busy city centre roundabout!

Weren't we lucky and if that weren't good enough our view was hampered by a few large trees directly in front and just when you think things can't get any better, as we sat down it decided to rain! It just seemed ironic that after all the miles we had clocked up today, we sat down for a few minutes' peace and relaxation right in the middle of one of the busiest junctions we'd seen since we'd set off.

We were joking around about the view. I remember Edd commenting on how I bring him to all the best places and how I couldn't have picked a better view, well it wouldn't have been hard!

So, we sat there for a rest and had a bite or two and topped up on our fluids. I think it was the longest I'd ever stopped so far. Edd seemed to have an endless supply of goodies in his bag. I remember wondering what was going to come out next.

Unlike myself he is so used to camping and the outdoor living and seemed so well prepared to get by without the use of the shops and garages that I relied on. He sat there making up some kind of wrap with an assortment of non-perishable food he'd brought with him.

I've never done camping myself. I often wonder what it would be like and often wished I'd have done it for my children when they were younger, just for the hell of it. My wife's never been keen either, four/five-star hotel always sounds a bit more appealing to me and I know what she'd say.

I must say what really puts me off as well as the obvious uncomfortable sleeping arrangements is the cleansing and toilet side of it. I do like to feel clean, clean clothes, bath every day or at least a shower. I have been known to have three baths in a day and my record is four if I remember correctly.

Sounds crazy I know but I got up one Saturday morning, had a bath as I usually would if I weren't working, went to karate training, came back had another bath, drains were playing up out the front of the house and down the road, so after helping out there I had another bath, then I had a fourth bath at the end of the day before I went to bed!

And guess what, when I got up Sunday morning I had another bath, so I guess that could have actually been five baths in twenty-four hours!

Anyway, so there we were sitting at this roundabout in Exeter city centre having lunch in the pouring rain, enjoying the view, probably looked like a couple of bells on a bench to every passer-by and typically the minute lunch was over, the rain decided to stop. Someone up there was definitely having a laugh with us!

As we marched off again, my feet and ankles were a bit on the stiff side which was one of the problems of stopping so long, so slow start again as we set off. As we cleared our way out of the city and back out towards the countryside, I was beginning to pick up pace and mentally prepared for the afternoon slog to Newton Abbott, our next port of call.

Marching up one of the minor roads and we were in head on collision with a major dual carriageway again. Immediately ahead of us the road gave way to a gradient making its way up to a bridge crossing the carriageway and allowing access to both sides. As the gradient took hold my pace only strengthened.

Just like walking the hills yesterday I seemed more comfortable under foot than walking flats and down the slopes. As I marched on forward, I was increasing distance between myself and Edd, Problem was that Edd was now navigating so unless he got a spurt on my push forward would be in vain.

As I neared the top, towards, the bridge, I was looking back anxiously awaiting instruction from Edd as to whether I was to proceed forward or veer right and cross the bridge. As I came to rest at the bridge, I was chuffed to bits that I'd picked up the pace again, only to be disheartened to have to come to a complete stand still while I waited for Edd to catch up.

Just couldn't understand why he hadn't pushed the pace with me, he was fresh, this was his first day, yes, he may be the silent tortoise that plods along at a steady pace and consequently passing the hare that raced up ahead and burnt out of steam but in my mind, I was in dire need of support and wasting the energy I'd just exerted was clearly not in my favour.

He was still unsure when he reached us, turning on the satnav as he arrived and having to wait for it to load. I'd become a dab hand at dealing with the route up until now and would always have the route planned before I hit the next junction, never did I walk to a point and decided later, I just didn't have the time for that.

I had to stay calm which is easy to say if my feet weren't feeling so dam sore again. It was almost easier to walk round in circles than to stop and go through the pain each time of getting going again. It wasn't just the pain either, it was also the time factor, reaching our destination at the earliest time I could make it, not his pace but mine.

What I mean by that is I needed him to support me, speed up when I was pushing forward and wait for me when I was struggling. My feet had now done about 200 miles and were far from in great shape. The thought that every time I gained some time it would be lost again or just thrown away as he lagged behind was mentally crippling to me.

I couldn't show my anger, well to be honest it was more frustration really. We'd been mates for so many years I certainly weren't going to fall out over something as trivial as that. It was a frustration being driven by the pain in my feet but I was mentally strong and this was just another angle being thrown at me. I was never going to give up, not now, not in the coming days.

We crossed the bridge and dropped down onto the carriageway, the usual way facing the oncoming traffic, right back onto a major road again. As I straddled the tarmac at the roads edge Edd lunged his way through the long grasses of the unforgiving verges. The road ahead once again began to climb and as I took it on with all the stamina and grit I could muster, I was doing real justice to miles left ahead.

Edd's pace seemed casual behind me. As I pushed on regardless once again the gap seemed to widen, a bit further and a bit further and a bit further. Hopefully he was going to catch me up soon, surely he would catch me up as it levelled out and started to descend. But as I trudged on the gradient just kept rising.

I remember seeing a huge carriageway swing right over the top of us and veer off to the left-hand side. In the back of my mind, I must admit a small part of me was questioning should we be on that route but not doubting the route we were on, I had full confidence in Edd; this had to be right.

I eventually got to a point and stopped, what if I was to get too far ahead and miss the route where we needed to branch off. I could no longer see Edd behind me. Losing him now would be a disaster for me, he had my satnav. The road behind had veered round at an angle and Edd was nowhere to be seen.

I called him on my mobile but received no reply. I think it was at that point where I noticed a few missed calls on my phone. He must have tried to call me but his calls had gone unheard as the traffic thundered past. I had no choice but to start walking back down the carriageway towards him.

I just remember feeling so frustrated, a chance to gain time, a chance to knock down some mileage, all scuppered and all efforts wasted. Walking down hill for me was quite painful so gaining time walking up was of such importance.

This was my first day with Edd and things weren't panning out too perfectly. I gritted my teeth and remained calm; I had no choice. I was now 200 miles into a 335 mile walk and all I could focus on was reaching my destination for the day, just as I'd got through every other day so far.

As I caught back up with Edd, I don't think he was too impressed either that I'd wandered on so far. I really think he just didn't get it. I just had to accept that he didn't fully understand or appreciate me pushing so hard whenever I could, why would he!

My feet were starting to get really uncomfortable again. I think I'd reached a peak of fitness with them yesterday and now I was about to push them too far. They were crying out for rest but I wasn't listening.

Edd seemed a bit puzzled as he checked from map to map, comparing the satnav to his phone in his hand and paper maps alike. I don't think I could have felt any lower when I heard him say, thinking out loud.

*"I think we might have taken the wrong turn back there?"*

My heart sank, the last thing I needed was extra miles to walk and extra hours on my feet. I say he thought out loud as I really don't believe he meant to say it, as he played it down as if it gave way to trivial consequences.

I guess if I put myself in his shoes a few miles out of the way were nothing in the scale of things but I can assure you if your feet were as bad as mine, you'd look at things a wee bit differently. Little things like that were big things and I needed them like a hole in the head. I just kept calm and as they say, 'carried on regardless.

Once again, we were soon off the main carriageway and walking the country lanes of Devon, passing through tiny villages with trivial populations and winding through the narrow country lanes addressed with hedgerows on both sides and the odd clearing which gave way to a few sheep or cows in a field or a farmhouse or two.

Unlike yesterday the hedge rows were high and the views obscured but at least we were away from that blasted traffic with its choking fumes and drowning noise.

We eventually re-joined the carriageway as we drew ever closer to Newton Abbott. A few miles further and we were off again, walking the urban streets of the town centre that lie ahead. One thing I do remember was stopping at a garage shortly before reaching the Inn. I'd ask Edd to pick up a small pot of milk for tea.

I have vivid memories of this garage in my head as I wondered round in circles on the forecourt as it was less painful on my feet rather than stopping and getting going again. The guy in the shop must have thought I was some kind of lunatic marching round and round his forecourt as I waited for Edd. To be quite honest, he probably wasn't far wrong!

The last half mile seemed never ending and I no longer had the satnav at hand to count down the yards as I had done previously. I couldn't wait to reach our destination, take the weight off my feet and put another day behind us. Just to really top the day off this was the first one I had stopped in with no ground floor reception.

I had to climb a mountain to reach it, well actually just one flight of stairs but it felt worse. And weren't we lucky to get the most miserable, arrogant receptionist of all so far! Employee of the month with no doubt! No smile, no eye contact, no conversation and no expression other than making us feel that we were putting him out, so sorry to trouble him!

Maybe we should have walked 30 miles back in the same direction we had come from where we were made to feel so welcome. People like that don't deserve to be employed, well certainly not dealing with the public anyway. I always like to give people the benefit of the doubt but I think he was just a rude man. I came back down to reception room to make a phone call as the reception in my room was quite poor.

As I sat there in the corner, just a few feet away from his desk, he couldn't even acknowledge my existence. If I was that miserable in life, I don't think I'd bother getting up in the morning. I think I'd just pop my own nails in the box and save everyone the miserable face.

Back up to the room, cleaned up and sorted out and got ourselves over to the restaurant for dinner. My feet were half crippling me yet again, it'd been another long day. I sat in the restaurant and chilled out over a couple of drinks, Edd on the larger and me on the hard stuff, lemonade or Pepsi! It had been quite a day.

Back to an early start tomorrow, similar distance again as we'd done today. Next stop was Plymouth or Plymouth East to be precise. I still remember Edd's face when I told him what time I was setting the alarm for but he was cool with it, especially when realising what time, we had finally arrived this evening.

To me getting away a bit earlier and having at least five and a half miles less to drag myself was quite a pleasing thought. No more distances over 30 miles and only two more really long days left.

It was almost beginning to feel like the worst was over, like it was almost reachable, like I was really going to make it all the way down, just as I'd promised myself when I set off from London, if only it was! If only!

# Chapter 13
# The Saw Mill

Mon 20<sup>th</sup> June. Up and out early again this morning, good old stint ahead of us again, 28.8 miles to East Plymouth. By tonight we'd almost be at the border of Cornwall. One thing I was really looking forward to was crossing the Tamar Bridge. Up early, done all my usual chores, feet lubricated and wrapped up.

I'd also been putting Sudocrem on them in the evening to soothe them and help keep them sterile. Had breakfast and looked forward to getting out of this miserable old place and on to a much more welcoming one.

As it turned out, it wasn't just the Inn where people seemed far from upbeat, which is the kindest way to put it. We walked away from the Inn and our walk took us directly through the centre of town.

Now I know it was Monday morning and people everywhere were busy with minds occupied with getting to work and school or whatever they were doing and it may have been a little drizzly and damp that morning can't remember now but what I do remember was everybody's face or more to the point not seeing anyone's face.

Everyone was walking along with their heads to the ground, not a single eye contact with a single person, so not a single good morning or shake of the head or nod of anything. After gradually coming away further and further from London, I was getting quite use to friendly folk that would readily pass the time of day with a cheeky grin or the wink of an eye or a good morning to you but not here.

No, it just wasn't going to happen, too much of an effort it would appear. I was sort of guessing now but the chap that worked in the reception at the Inn was obviously a local lad. You get towns, villages etc. where it just seems to rub off from one person to another, whether it be happy or sad.

This was certainly not one of those happy places, I mean I may be wrong but that was my impression after my night's stay and my short visit through town. Even my experience in one of the small convenience stores was much the same. To be honest the staff seemed quite rude.

It felt a little bit like being in the land of 'Shaun of the Dead', anyway not really my problem, I didn't have to live there. Edd was laughing at me, whether he agreed with me or not I'm not quite sure, maybe he was just in an argumentative mood or maybe there was some kind of bug in the air there. As a sociable person, I could feel the tension and I was glad we were moving on.

Today turned out to be a great day as far as the route was concerned. An enormous amount of the route turned out to be off the beaten track and right in the heart of the Devonshire countryside. It also turned out to be a very trying day physically with memories that I will never forget and memories I will always cherish!

Wasn't long before we were out of the town and out on to the A381. Just a short distance down here before we branched off into unspoilt countryside. Just in case anyone is interested in the actual route, Conniford Lane to be precise. It was great to get away from the speeding traffic and on to these single-track lanes, with peace and tranquillity and nature all around.

Rolling hills in the distance and above, birds of prey soaring through the sky. Hedgerows filled with beautiful butterflies, birds singing in the trees and bees as busy all around.

The early morning spring air was still refreshing on your face and the odd bleating from the distant sheep and sound from the cows breaking the silence as randomly as the sun popping through broken clouds scattered across the sky above.

There was also the occasional sound of a distant tractor and that lovely fresh smell of the true countryside, need I explain! What a joy to be walking dawn to dusk, no work, no car, no shopping, no running around doing the normal day to day chores.

If only I could have forgot about the pain in my feet it would have been like heaven or like some kind of dream of an idyllic new world but to be broken occasionally by the sound of an oncoming vehicle which was hard not to hear from a distance, so fair warning to move out of harm's way.

Talking about driving this was the longest I had ever been without driving my car or any kind of vehicle since I'd started driving at the age of seventeen.

With my wife not driving it's very rare for me to go even a day without getting into a car and driving somewhere.

Even when we go away on holiday, we usually hire a car wherever we go and we tend to travel a lot. I do find it quite amusing sometimes when you talk to people and they make out they seen the world over the years, going away on holidays here there and everywhere, then you get talking to them and about ninety percent of the places they've been, they never left the complex!

Then they have the nerve to laugh at you going back to the same place twice! Well, when we go to places, we like to explore and I mean explore a lot. I must admit we've spent a lot of time over the years visiting the Canary Isles and I reckon we've seen more of the Canaries than a lot of the people that live there.

Mind this is quite typical. I spent a lot of my childhood life looking out of my bedroom window, looking out towards Windsor Castle and people visit the castle from all over the world and can probably tell you a dam site more about its history than I can.

Anyway, back to our walk. We were by now well away from the town and we had a few miles under our belt and in need of a short stop. It can be pretty hard at times finding convenient places to stop in places like these so you just have to take advantage of any opportunity you see.

As we veered left at one of the junctions from one narrow lane to another, a golden opportunity was just staring us in the face. Lovely little cottage on the corner on our left-hand side. As we strolled past this property, we noticed a layby type arrangement and there at the leading edge behind us were crazy pathing steps leading up to a well-established conifer and beyond that you could just make out a beautiful flower garden laid to a neatly trimmed lawn.

It looked like a very respectable property, the building itself a quaint cottage type construction painted white. There was a name board on the side of the cottage which I will choose not to reveal and the property opposite had an entrance which led out directly onto the junction. The steps looked so tempting.

Surely, they wouldn't mind if we parked ourselves down for a short while, I mean what harm we could be doing. Had they been pottering around outside I would of jolly well ask them and half desperate for a quick break as we were, we were almost tempted to tap on their door out of politeness.

I'm sure I do remember now seeing a chap in the garden opposite acknowledge us, so seemingly a friendly neighbourhood and for sure he would know his neighbours being so isolated as they were.

We decided we weren't doing any harm. We really didn't want to disturb them so we both just decamped our large bags and took five. I remember those steps as if it were yesterday.

Didn't stop for too long for we had a fair distance to cover. Still following the satnav now religiously we came upon a place further up with conflicting access in the direction we were heading.

Up until now I must say the satnav had been absolutely fantastic and the routes it has sent us up from day to day had been absolutely brilliant, totally reliable and very varied, so it'd been an interesting trip so far. Up until now we had not got lost or ended up at any kind of dead end or unpassable lane or way.

The road ahead forked off into two slightly different directions. We followed the planned route to the right which all seemed well until reaching a gate ahead and a small sign attached which read to the effect of *'private land, no right of way'*.

Now I've seen all this before far too often on country walks, landowners taking the law into their own hands, doing their best to deter would be walkers from passing across their land despite footpaths and bylaws that have allowed public access for centuries. Even putting up physical barriers like barbed wire fencing and beware of the guard dog signs. They try it all!

What were we to do now! We were now in a bit of a dilemma, do we carry on regardless and take the risk of what lie ahead or find an alternative route, which is not quite so easy when you're on foot. All ok in a car, you do a few miles down an alternative road, it doesn't work out, you turn round and come back and you've only wasted five minutes but on foot, just a bit different.

We decided to turn back, go back to the fork in the road and take the left turn. Not sure how this was going to affect our mileage but surely if we just kept right, it would put us back on route further up somewhere, well that was the plan anyway.

We weren't the only ones to be caught out, as we turned back a delivery van done exactly the same as us and thinking we might be local, ask us for help. I'm sure he would have found his way somehow.

Of course, as we forked off to the left the satnav kept telling us to turn back and follow the same route until we got far enough down the road, then it reset and bingo! We were back in business, with not too many more miles added.

The lanes became much narrower, the hedges taller and the hills steeper. The lane got to a point where any approaching vehicle would have to wait for us to find a convenient point amongst the hedges before passing by.

Any vehicle wider than six foot six would surely not be able to pass through now with ease, we may have passed a sign to that effect I really don't recall now. Even the tarmac would disappear in places giving way to almost dirt gravel tracks with allotments of weeds and grasses growing through the centre of the road as conditions deteriorated.

The height of the hedges here would tower above your head and restrict most views of the rolling slopes of the land around.

I had to stop and plaster myself in insect repellent as I was starting to get bitten quite frequently from the abundance of midges and insects which seemed to be closing in on us. It was like walking into a lion's den but in the miniature world, so instead of one big bite around your neck, about a thousand small ones and as much blood removed as each individual could indulge itself.

I'd left the magic repellent off after learning my lesson a few times before being blinded by chemicals running in my eyes in the face of any shower. Time for my revenge as I stopped and coated up.

I encouraged Edd to use some as well, it was essential. The stuff really was magical, a few sprays of that stuff was like having some kind of mysterious force field around you, physically keeping them at bay.

There was a group of horses ahead slowly making their way up towards us. Being so narrow we really didn't want to take any chances down the side of them, not when there was a perfect gap in the fence close by. We pulled aside and awaited the approaching gang.

They were certainly in no rush; in fact I don't think they could have crawled along any slower had they been tied to the front of a tractor with the handbrake on. I guess they were just enjoying the leisurely pace of the countryside and why not. I must admit they were all polite enough when they did pass, eventually!

We'd crossed beneath a railway line and this lane was heading back towards the railway once again, which sort of made sense as railway lines often take the shortest route between places or close enough.

The road meandered down and cut beneath a low dark dingy old arched bridge as we crossed beneath the lines. Not the sort of place you would want to hang around too long, and certainly not on a dark winter's evening.

We passed a tiny school, St Christopher's Prep School and Nursey. Literally just a couple of small buildings and a carpark with a handful of cars parked out front. I've often wondered what it would be like to attended a school like that. I went to a much bigger school.

In fact, I went to two infant schools as a new one was built half way through my time attending the first. Following that I moved onto a middle school that was huge in comparison to some schools and even that was split into two different buildings at two separate locations.

So, by the time I went to my last school, I'd already effectively been to four different schools which were all quite large. Regardless to your education I can only imagine the difference between a tiny school and a huge school must have a huge difference on the social skills you learn.

I guess it could also have a negative effect as well as I can only imagine a lot more bullying goes on in a larger school, which can have life lasting effects on some people. My boys are lucky as apparently the school they go to doesn't have any bullying problems, well apparently anyway! Did you see that fly over then!

Further up the track we met up with the railway again but this time it was a level crossing. Of course, the gates were down and the red lights on, you know how it goes! Mind it wasn't your average level crossing. It was quite an idyllic one to say the least and a quaint little station too.

As it goes it was quite a joy to stop and to admire one of Britain's finest steam trains passing through. I was so busy admiring the train in the flesh I didn't think to get my phone out and take a few snaps of it.

By the time I decided to do so, in my haste to get the perfect shot, sods law my phone managed to switch itself off and by the time I got it back up and working again I barely caught the end of the last carriage as it chuffed its way out of the station.

Beyond the level crossing we crossed a meanderings river via a beautiful historic stone bridge. With its low walls and multiple triangular parapets and stunning naturalistic views in both directions we took a few moments to take in the stunning surroundings. Today the true British countryside really did seem to close in on us with a pure surreal feeling.

My feet were really feeling it again today and despite the enjoyment of taking in our remarkable surroundings I was counting down the miles left to go. Not having control of the satnav, I was counting down the miles in my head then I'd ask Edd just occasionally on the ETA and a mileage check.

I'd try my best to be over generous with the miles so as to give myself a pleasant surprise but that could sometimes mentally backfire when you found you'd actually covered less ground than you thought you had, not realising the pace had slowed so much.

I remember seeing signs for Rattery. The signs seemed to go on for ever. It probably wasn't all that far but it sure felt like it to me. It was quite a trying day if I recall with barely a flat bit of land to walk. The hills I could handle but the slopes just crippled my feet every time, each step getting more and more painful as I descended.

As time passed by finding somewhere suitable to stop for lunch seemed to be an impossible task. Lane after lane, bend after bend but nothing but hedgerows and high grasses, thistles and nettles and everything but. I think there was more chance of finding a dodo!

As we walked on leaving Rattery well behind us, for a split second my eagle eye caught sight of what appeared to be something sticking out from behind a hedge, which had some kind of resemblance to an actual proper seat.

Was I seeing things or was my mind just playing tricks on me, like being in a desert and seeing a thirst-quenching oasis only to find when you get there it was just a mirage. I stopped in my tracks.

*"Hang on a minute, Edd!"* I exclaimed, *"I'm sure I just spotted something."* I backed up a few feet to where the road had just split in two and sure enough, I was right. There amongst the hedge rows was a gated entrance to some kind of builder's yard type premises and sure enough just sticking out from a hedge on

the right-hand side was a real table and benches just screaming out for someone to sit on them.

Though it was just a glimpse of a piece of wood sticking out there was something about the height, shape and thickness of it that just screamed out to me 'BENCH'. The gates were wide open. It was an old sawmill, with work in progress.

If I remember right there were a few timber worktops scattered around on the left-hand side and further back and some kind of office to the right, just past this most desirable seat. Can't say I've ever been so excited to see a wooden table and benches.

*"That was a good spot, Edd!"* I said, but clearly Edd's face was not quite as clear about the next few moments as mine was.

*"It's on their premises mate,"* he replied. I really didn't care where it was. The way my legs felt I would have rugby tackled anyone who got within inches of my way of stopping me reaching it.

My mind was already sitting there relaxing before my body had even entered the gates. It was a proper bench with a shelter, it was like an open-air canteen.

I involuntary hobbled through the gates and on to site and straight up to one of the lads working there

*"Excuse me bud,"* I said *"excuse me, this might sound like a crazy request but we've been walking for miles and miles and haven't sat down for hours, we couldn't just rest up on your bench for a short while, could we?"*

To be quite frank, I didn't really have a clue what the answer was going to be but I sure knew what the right answer was. I can't imagine anyone has ever strolled into their yard before and held them to siege over their bench. Well, there's always a first time!

Fortunately, the chap obliged, I was so relieved and so was Edd, relieved to sit down and take a break and relieved that we didn't have to start World War three over a bench. Thinking about it, tucked out the way in the middle of nowhere anything could have happened.

Ten lads could have jumped out from one of the workshops. For all we knew there could have been some kind of underground, black market business going on there disguised under the cover of a saw mill and we'd just stumbled onto their premises!

There were more lads as it goes, turned out to be a nice bunch and it was a proper saw mill, I think! We were told we could park ourselves down but not for long, not that they didn't want us sitting there but they were all about to shoot off for lunch in about five minutes time and the gates would have to be locked up.

Sure enough, after about five, we were kicked out the yard but that couldn't be helped. There outside the gates in a small layby opposite was an open backed truck. The lads were all shooting off but the truck was remaining there. One of the lads was so kind to us.

*"You can perch yourself on me open back truck if you like, take a rest as long as you like, sit and have your lunch there."*

As I said, we really did meet some charming people along the way and this was one of the moments I've never forgotten. There we were, sitting sprawled out on the back this truck, I tell you what, I could have curled up and crashed out for an hour easily!

It was great to take the weight off my feet, let them dangle over the side for a bit. Edd took a few snaps while we were there. We were joking around again about having a series of photos on different forms of transport, like the digger one and now catching a lift on the back of a truck.

Well, we couldn't stay too long, we still had a fair old way to track. The biggest problem with stopping again was getting going. Putting that rucksack back on my back was like somebody tying my shoulders down to the ground with some kind of elasticated ropes and gradually putting the pressure back on my feet as I took the first few steps, like somebody smacking the soles of my feet with strong bamboo canes as a punishment.

I could sort of gauge the soreness of my feet by the angle I was placing them down. The worse my feet became the more the angle I would position them and the smaller my strides became, I then had to push on through the pain gradually building up speed and lengthening my strides.

It really did feel like a tough day and things were just about to take a turn for the worse. Heading on towards a small town called Ivy Bridge I was to face a steep slope that nearly finished me off. Going downhill was never easy but this was a one in five gradient and seemed to go on and on, most likely due to the slow pace I was walking.

As I edged my way down towards a big railway arch near the bottom, my feet were screaming at me to stop. Every slow step as my feet were pushed hard against the front and side of my boots, depending how I was hobbling, was etching pain on my face. I couldn't stop, I had to keep going, I had to make it to the bottom of the hill, at least then I could rest again and relieve the pain from my feet somehow.

With the steepness of the slope and the odd way I was walking to compensate for the pain as I clutch my stick, the film around my feet had moved to a point where it was now snagging hard between my toes and felt like someone driving a blade up between them.

I reached the bottom. There at the very bottom of the slope at the t junction, my prayers were answered. A small green bench next to a bus stop. I just had to sit down, sit down and recompose myself. I gentle pulled my boots from my feet and socks and film to reveal my angry feet.

I recovered them with copious amounts of Vaseline them rewrapped them. I had plenty of Vaseline in my bag, I'd requested Edd to bring a big pot with him and save the jokes for later. I've heard them all before. I rewrapped my feet and gently squeezed them into my boots.

Fully aware that the clock was ticking and I'd just wasted another whole lot of time sorting out my feet as well as the pace I'd been pushing or not rather, I noticed that Edd was checking the time more and more frequently. He was not impressed with the pace, I could tell.

Physically I needed to stop, mentally I just couldn't even if it meant dragging myself along the path inch by inch and arriving by midnight at the Inn, I just had to keep moving!

Then all in a brief moment, everything changed. Edd looked at me with a bewildering look on his face. I could see his mind was working overtime, wondering how we were going to get through all this. He'd now been walking with me for nearly two days and with four days still ahead of us, he could see I would be struggling.

He'd planned time off work, booked his hotel at Land's End, paid for the rail tickets home, prepared himself for his own gruelling part of the walk and all was coming crashing to an end so quickly.

*"Have you tried a paracetamol?"* He asked. I must admit it hadn't ever occurred to me. Why would it? I don't take tablets unless I have to, I've never liked taking tablets unless considered totally necessary.

As I already said, I was on a strong dose of ibuprofen anyway to try to limit the swelling on my left ankle but taking paracetamol as well is something I hadn't even thought about until now. I know you can take them together and I believe they are more effective when you do but never have done before.

*"That might be an idea,"* I replied, not realising he had some in his bag with him. I took two. Surely, they would make some difference, I mean I rarely take them, so my bodies not used to them so hopefully they would be very effective.

Wasn't expecting instant relief but sure enough they did help. Clutching my stick, I rose to my feet and began my steady shuffle forward. As I built up speed and lengthened my stride, to my amazement the usual pain gradually bit by bit started to fade away, almost without notice as I pushed on further down the road, I was relieved from most of the pain altogether.

Our pace increased as we strode through Ivy Bridge and beyond and as we marched back onto the minor country lanes we were now flying along. This was one of the best speeds I had pushed for days. We were now making good time towards Plymouth, even gaining time on our estimated arrive.

As we closed the last few miles my feet were starting to tingle again. It had been a long day and I couldn't wait to get there. I remember stopping at a large garage in the closing miles for a few more pick me ups including another Red Bull.

Edd waited on a little wall along by the footpath on the edge of the forecourt. I could see he had not been impressed today and there I was stopping again. I was ages in the garage, there was a small que in front of me and can't exactly remember what the problem was now but something was causing a major delay.

I was standing in the que marching my feet so as to keep them moving and being looked upon though I was some kind of nutter escaped from Broadmoor.

Further up the road, I do remember us having a laugh when we sat on a low-level wall for a quick drink break and in my tiredness allowed my sack to pull me backwards, clean off the wall with my legs in the air. I had to unclip the straps on my bag and free myself just to be able to sit back up and then reload again after.

A little further up and we were literally down to the last few miles when Edd saved the day again, as my battery died on the satnav. He pulled out a battery backup he'd brought for his phone and managed to guide us the final leg. The satnav battery had failed today for the first time, partly because Edd had it switched on so much and partly because we'd had such a long day I suppose.

I had the settings on real low to conserve as much power as possible. I had the voice turned down to nothing and the brightness down to trivial percent which I must admit did have its problems in bright sunlight some times.

Main thing was we made it and before dark, well just about. It was a good job I'd planned all this for the longest days of the year. Another day over and still holding on in there!

Arriving so late meant less time for my poor old feet to recover and as the tablets wore off and the pain gradually returned, I gave in two more tablets for a good night sleep. So, so looking forward to tomorrow, only 19.5 miles to Liskeard, what a relief, my easiest stretch by far since the second day, Bagshot to Basingstoke.

Today had been a real long one. Even my wife was surprised at how late I called as I would usually call her every evening when I reached the Inn. Really looking forward to crossing the Tamar Bridge in the morning and into the final county, Cornwall.

# Chapter 14
# Dinner for Two

Tuesday 21st June. A day I'll never forget. Had a really great day today as it turned out. Met a member of the public today that was so thoughtful and what he did, so unexpected! Memories I'll always cherish.

Up out of bed this morning as optimistic as ever that my feet would be on the mend. Of course, in all honesty that was going to be most unlikely. One saving grace was that my little toe didn't seem to be quite so painful any more. I wonder if it was the increased severity of the rest of my feet that was distracting my mind or maybe it had actually settled down a bit.

Had four more days to go and only one real long stretch which was tomorrow. Still couldn't contemplate not finishing this walk, I just had to do it somehow.

Set off after breakfast a bit slow as expected but with the relief in mind that today was a much shorter distance, so not only less pain but hopefully tonight I would get a bit more rest, a bit more well-needed recovery time. My feet were still twisting inwards which was frustrating, if only I could place my feet flat down on the ground and walk normally.

I'd now clocked up over 243 miles, most of which I'd limped my way along. I'd looked forward to today. I was so looking forward to crossing the Tamar Bridge, a great milestone to reach.

First part of our journey today was not the most relaxing, pretty much the urban streets of the outskirts of Plymouth until we crossed over into Cornwall, where from there onwards it was much more rewarding as we cut our way through the heart of the lush countryside once again.

Very first step was navigating a short stretch of the main A30 dual carriageway once again. For the first time we actually split up and went our separate ways and came together again at the next junction.

Edd had his carriageway phobia head on again and refused to walk the short distance up to the next point. I think it may have only been about half a mile, it may have been even less than that. He'd been looking on his phone and checking an alternative route to the satnav.

The last thing I was going to do was to add more miles to today's journey regardless to how little, plus of course I didn't want to encourage him. If we'd have taken the long route here who knows what he'd have planned for me further up. So, we both crossed the carriageway together then split off our separate ways.

As it turned out there was a very safe path that run the whole distance of this carriageway, all the way up to the next turn off, so there was really no need for Edd to have gone off in the end whatsoever. Maybe a 150 mile walk just wasn't enough for him. Maybe he needed to do 158 and a half or something like that!

Truth be known, I think it was more of that man thing we all have inside us. You know, the 'you're not telling me what to do and I'll prove it!' Well, I certainly couldn't condemn him there because if I said I was only a little bit like that, I'd be lying!

Anyway, so I got to the roundabout, top of the road, just off the dual carriageway and of course then had to wait for Edd to catch up. Six hours later! No, only joking but his route did take longer naturally.

Over the next few miles, I remember walking up hill a fair bit and one thing that really sticks in my mind was just how urban it was. Housing after housing after housing. It was like walking through one big, giant housing estate.

I still remember having a quick chat as I passed a local, about the steepness of the hill on one particular road, joking around about how it kept her fit. Passed a local shop and stopped for some supplies, this time I also purchased a packet of paracetamol, I'd been pinching them off Edd until now.

Got a quick glimpse of the Tamar Bridge when we were within about a mile of it then it somehow disappeared out of view. Then you start questioning the satnav but it always comes up trumps every time.

As we climbed the summit of our last little slope it seemed to just spring out of nowhere. One second the bridge was nowhere to be seen, the next it was towering above us in all its glory.

I was so thrilled to have reached this point, it really was a major milestone in my head and a mental boost to spur us on. The magnificent bridge stood proud in front of us with its spectacular views of the surrounding landscape and estuary on both sides.

To the south lie an old wrought iron railway bridge which I would be using on my way back home. Edd shot off to the little boys' room which was great. I don't mean great for him mind he was probably quite relieved but great for me, for once again I was waiting for him, not him waiting for me.

Saying that, second time today after the roundabout earlier. While he done his business, I took the opportunity to take a short rest and sit and admire the suspension bridge, eagerly awaiting to proceed across.

Over the bridge and goodbye Devon, hello Cornwall and Land's End here we come! We crossed the bridge and continued to walk through Saltash. As we walked up through Saltash high street I received a text again from Robert. This time I had the pleasure of sending a message back to say I'd just crossed the Tamar Bridge and I was now in Cornwall.

Ready for a short break we kept an eye out for somewhere convenient to stop. Can't exactly remember why now but for some reason we decided to walk right up and out the other side of the high street before stopping. As it was this decision turned out to be one of the best things we ever done!

Just after the high street on the right-hand side of the road was a small park, overlooking the estuary and back across to Devon. There just down a small bit from one of the entrances was a very welcoming bench enticing us in for lunch.

So glad we stopped there that day as what happened next was the start of a much unexpected event!

We sat down, made ourselves as comfortable as we could, mind I don't think my feet were ever going to feel perfect, not in fact for a long time. The park with its lush green grass and sparse trees was quite open and as the land sloped away in front of us it gave way to some amazing views to admire.

Still remember Edd joking about bringing him to a better place for lunch today. It was gradually improving every day. The first day was the roundabout in Exeter followed by the back of a truck yesterday and now today looking out across the estuary at the open countryside.

Anyway, so this smartly dressed gentleman came wondering past with his dog and as you do, passed the time of day with some light chat, you know the usual things, weather, views, etc. He was a local chap very local indeed as he lived across the road from where we were sitting. I had the charity bib on and of course with the obvious large rucksacks we both had we very quickly got talking about what we were up to.

The gentleman then seemed to have a lot of admiration for what we were doing and talked about making a donation. It was always nice to bump into people like this, just reminded you what a great cause you were doing it for and spurred you on to continue. Lovely chap, very friendly too.

Well, we finished our lunch and got back on route. Got a few miles down the road and this car pulls up beside us both. What happened next, we simple wasn't expecting but one of the most memorable moments of the whole walk. So, this car pulls up and down comes this window. Expecting someone to ask for directions or something, we both approached the driver.

*"Hi again lads,"* he said. It was the same gentleman we'd been talking to not so long ago back in the park. *"I understand you're heading for the Liskeard Premier Inn."*

*"That's right,"* I answered. Well surely, he wasn't offering us a lift as he knew we had to walk.

*"What's your favourite tucker guys?"*

I can't now remember the exact words he said but basically, he was asking what we liked to eat. I think a nice steak meal was mentioned by one of us in the conversation, it may well have even been him suggesting it.

*"I'm heading that way!"* He exclaimed, *"When you get there lads, there'll be a tab behind the bar for you in the restaurant, have a nice meal on me!"*

Quite taken back.

*"Thanks,"* we both replied. Then he shot off! Well to be honest we were both a bit stunned by the gentleman's unexpected generosity and thoughtfulness. It seemed so out of the blue we almost didn't want to believe it for not building up false hopes. I mean it's not every day a complete stranger not only offers to buy you diner but puts themselves out of their way to do it as well. We were both amazed, almost in shock!

We got back to reality and continued on our travels. Out onto the main road once again but before long we spurred off onto a nice country lane. Country lanes all the way from now on, it was a most enjoyable afternoon. We walked up passed Notter Bridge Inn, then straight up turning into Frenchman's Lane.

It was a steep hill and seemed to go on for ever and a day. The lane was really narrow, just about as wide as an average car with steep banks on both sides which gave way to fresh greenery growing in the shade of the overhanging trees and bushes. Ivy clinging to the banks and in some place's thick clumps of long grasses, nettles and ferns.

Dark in places till we reached nearer the top with barely room to escape any approaching traffic if the need occurred. I was trudging up like a machine to the top, pushing and pushing and using my stick to pull me up with pure determination and spirit. I don't think we walked a flat bit of ground the entire day.

As we neared the top, the lane started to flatten out and we were back out into the glare of the sun, sweating as the heat burned through. It was always hard to feel completely comfortable when the sun was out. This time of year, the sun can feel very hot and although you could strip down a bit the thick cushioning between the rucksack and your back would soon heat up and make you feel sweaty.

Other than chatting to another man with his dogs further up the lane as it levelled out, I can't say much else happened today that I remember. Just this guy parked up on a strip of lawn, holding back his dogs in his car and cracking some joke and general chit chat as we walked on by.

We had made real steady pace all afternoon and were looking forward to reaching the Premier Inn in good time. My feet had survived another day but only thanks to the paracetamol I was now on. I was taking the tablets every four hours as suggested and at times counting the hours in between as I could feel the pain returning as the tablets wore off.

All afternoon I'd been looking forward to an earlier finish, finally some rest time for my feet and what about this tab behind the bar when we got there, was it for real? Not that we doubted this gentleman at all but it just seemed a little surreal.

We arrived at the reception to a very warm welcome indeed! This gentleman had been in ahead of us and sure enough had put a tab behind the bar. He'd been in to the reception and the staff were aware of us on our way!

The young girls behind the desk, I think one of them was called Vicky if I remember right but can't be certain now, anyway she was so kind, she even got us booked into a room close to reception knowing how far we'd been walking. If things couldn't get any better today the girls even offered to do some washing for us!

Well, that was grand, saying that we'd spent over a grand with them so I suppose it wasn't really breaking their budget with a bit of extra customer service in return. We were chuffed to bits to get some socks and pants put through the wash. I was particularly pleased to get some more clean socks.

I'd left home with what I thought to be a workable system of sock rotation to last me the full duration of my trip but thanks to the storm and a few occasions of my feet sweating a bit more than normal, largely due to the continuous hours of walking, I was running a little low on fresh socks.

I was delighted with the offer but had to explain, this was all well and good providing the washing came back to us in a dry condition. Not that beggars can be choosers and all that but a bag full of wet washing the following day really wasn't going to be ideal for us, as we had enough weight to carry as it was. She assured us all would be sorted by morning, so that was great!

We both got booked into our room and sorted out a large sack of washing between us. I took it down to reception and gingerly handed it over. Not too sure if the young girl knew what she was letting herself in for.

*"You might want to keep it at arm's length when you put it onto the machine!"* I suggested. We had a bit of a joke about the state of the washing, except I wasn't joking! That poor girl, I don't suppose she'll do that again in a hurry.

What a fantastic reception we'd arrived to. Just a bit better than the service we'd received a couple of nights back, back at Newton Abbott or should I say lack of service!

Tried to call my wife again that evening but reception here was so bad that I gave up and sent a text hoping it would get through eventually, explaining the poor reception and we'd talk again tomorrow. All was fine!

We had a great relaxing evening and both in high spirits for the very kind gesture of our meal. It wasn't the cost of it, more the fact that a complete stranger had put themselves out for us, completely voluntarily and totally out of the blue. This gentleman even came back later that evening and met up with us again in the restaurant, had another quick chat and wished us all the best on the rest of our trip.

Can't remember his name now, wish I could, never been brilliant with names and faces until I get to know somebody. Well just in case you are reading this, we'd both like to thank you once again for your kindness. I don't think I'll ever forget that evening!

Last big day ahead tomorrow, 29.3 miles, then two easier days to finish off. If I could only get through tomorrow, surely now I've cracked it!

# Chapter 15
# Newquay by Nightfall

Wednesday 22nd June. Had a long day ahead of us and I can tell you by the time we eventually reached Newquay, it really was a long one. First things first, popped down to reception to collect washing before breakfast and I must admit it came back a little more pleasant than it was when I handed it over. Had the full treatment from Liskeard Inn. Even had some bacon sandwiches made up for the road after breakfast.

We were in the restaurant as soon as it opened, needed to get back on the road as soon as we could. Still remember my feet feeling quite sore again despite the extra rest they'd had. Was a wee bit worrying really as my feet were gradually deteriorating day by day but my mind was still set on finishing what I'd started? Somehow, I just had to make it.

Set out limping with my feet dragging along at funny angles so not a good pace to start. As I said, going downhill was never good for me and I remember as I struggling down through the town with Edd ahead of me, I was wondering what was going through his mind as he patiently anticipated my speed.

We had almost 30 miles ahead of us today, ouch! I remember going down through some trees and along past some kind of industrial estate until following a main road for a bit then forking off.

As we forked off, it was a long straight road with no road marking and free from most traffic, just the odd passing vehicle of which you would get plenty of warning as the road laid so flat ahead and lacked in bends or deviation.

As we gradually built our distance from the main road the enjoyable tranquillity of the countryside was upon us once more again. Can't say I'm a fan of straight roads though I must say they always make for safer walking but can sometimes feel never ending.

The weather today was a bit unsettled and I'd resisted the use of the insect repellent for the fear of stinging my eyes again if it decided to rain. As we got deeper into the countryside it wasn't long before I was becoming dinner again to an army of hungry flying predators, so out came the repellent once again.

I also remember stopping along the route a few times for drinks and refuelling purposes and I can't be certain but I think my pace today was not that great at this point. I do remember Edd checking his watch quite regularly and readjusting our ETA in his head.

The miles just seemed to get longer and the end of the route just felt so far away. We eventually came to a gate which led straight into some beautiful national trust land. I must admit, I was a wee bit sceptical of the route we had taken.

Knowing how Edd desperately wanted to steer clear of the main roads and how seemingly so clued up he was on the route we had taken, it seemed he had taken us through this national trust land by his devious and clever navigational skills.

Looking back now it was complete fate and luck of the route we were on, of course I never doubted him for a second! I guess it was the pain in my feet that had tainted my mind that day. Not to worry.

We were in the grounds of an old Victorian house on the Lanhydrock Estate. The great house stands in extensive grounds, about 890acres and has been owned and managed by the national trust since 1953.

Much of the present house dates back to Victorian times but some even further back from the 1620s. It is set in beautiful gardens, most formal looking with its perfectly trimmed hedges and carefully positioned planned layout.

Before reaching the house, we followed a long straight path and I can honestly say it was probably the most people we had seen out walking for a long time. We found a nice bench to sit and take lunch.

Can't really remember now if it were actually lunch time or not, it may well have been lunch even though we'd not covered the number of miles we should have by now. Our estimated time of arrival was not looking good.

Nearly everyone passing by had a dog or two and I still remember someone's dog sniffing around me a bit closer than I wanted. Nothing against dogs at all but why do some people assume that just because they're a doggy person, everybody else likes dogs sniffing and licking them. I wouldn't have minded so much but I was trying to have my lunch.

The view today was really spectacular. I was joking with Edd about spoiling him as our lunch spot each day seemed to get better and better, not that it could ever of got any worse than that first one we shared on the middle of that roundabout.

We packed up, loaded up and set off once again. Passing the gracious Lanhydrock House and veering off the path from all the other walkers we eventually came to a small gateway which led us out of this national trust land and in not such a grand way as we'd entered it.

Felt a bit like slipping out the back door. This gateway led us straight out onto a small roundabout addressed by a few country roads and fairly scruffy hedgerows. What I did find amusing was sitting across the road on one of the small verges facing the junction was a little bench.

Proper little bench with arm rests and back. Even stretching my imagination, I couldn't think for one minute who would possibly want to sit there on the edge of this junction.

With its narrow paths, overgrown hedges and pure lack of space or views in any direction this just didn't seem like your average place you find a bench. Even looking back now on google it still looks a bit bizarre.

Shortly on from here and the clouds were becoming a bit more threatening, gradually gathering and gradually darkening and then the inevitable. Always a job to know how much it is going to rain and whether or not to stop and dress more appropriately.

You're warm and sweaty from the sun and a light shower in your face can be quite refreshing. Rain Mack on now might only make you feel hotter. Then of course if it decides to tip down and you're not wearing your water proofs then of course you get soaked through to the skin.

The worst thing that can happen is you put off covering up till you eventually decide you have to, too late you're soaked through, then it rains all day and you have soaking wet clothes under your raincoat, which really does feel knack!

Anyway, so we eventually stopped and covered up and of course so did the rain and a mile down the road there we were stripping off again. I guess I remember those moments not so much because of getting wet but more from that dam insecticide that would run down my face and sting my eyes to bits.

I had tried my best to avoid this situation today but didn't quite seem to succeed. Back on to the country lanes again with some great views as the land dropped away on one side. I do remember seeing that old steam train again in the far distance, assuming it was the same one we'd seen back at Tiverton Railway Station.

Once again trouble was looming ahead with my feet! Our pace today had slowed considerably and with the distance we had to cover this wasn't looking good. Hard to remember every little detail but I do remember how extremely sore and painful my feet had become.

I was running low on cling film and the small amount that I did have wrapped around my feet had become most uncomfortable. I was keeping myself topped up on the paracetamol on top of the ibuprofen but this was no longer able to mask the pain completely.

We came to a service station sort of area, a fairly new road layout crossing a main road with a few roundabouts and a garage forecourt close by with a shop. We navigated the junctions through and almost out the other side but I came to a grinding halt before moving on away and down the next route.

I'd just had about enough for the day! I sat down on the grass verge and pulled my boots clear from my feet. I was in no mood to walk another step, even the short distance over to the nearby shop. I could see the frustration building on Edd's face as he counted the minutes on to the end of our already long day.

*"Sorry bud but I just need something for my feet,"* I said. Edd could clearly see I was struggling and while I sat there and had a bit of a rest, he shot over to the shop for me with a small shopping list of essential items.

1) Cling film.

2) Chocolate or something similar.

3) Another can of Red Bull to give us a boost.

I sat and waited patiently for him and was delighted when he returned with a full order.

I got to work straight away on my feet, wrapping them plentifully with cling film and generous amounts of Vaseline beneath, smothering them from my toes right up past my ankles. I redressed with socks and boots taking great care to get the perfect tension on my laces. You wouldn't believe how important it was to get that right.

Topped up with some tablets, refuelled with some chocolate and downed the Red Bull. Somehow, I just had to keep moving forward, there was no other answer. I really needed that Red Bull to give me that extra boost of energy. Can't say I'm a fan of the stuff and haven't touched it since I've been back but it seemed to be a life saver at the time.

We set off at a slow pace as usual gradually building up speed. The first few steps were agony, it really did seem like mind over matter at times. We got up to a decent pace, I think Edd was quite surprised at our new found progress, considering how much pain I'd just been in.

Long straight road ahead again and I was steaming along fully aware that we needed to push the pace now and pull something out of the bag if we were to make it to Newquay by nightfall.

To think that on my third day I done 36 miles and knocked literally hours off today's pace, I must have been walking some pace that day. This walk and the deteriorating state of my feet really did seem to be taking its toll on me.

There was a layby ahead and parked up was a small car and a young woman besides it and she clearly looked in a bit of distress. She had a flat tyre, she needed help and it was soon to be dark. The last thing we needed right now was to stop and help someone as we were up against the clock ourselves plus of course I was in no fit state to really offer my assistance, given the pain I was in walking.

As we strolled past, the vulnerability and anxiety etched upon this young lady's face got the better of us and we both turned back to try to help. I know from my own experience that changing a wheel on the car can be an exercise that can require a fair bit of muscle to get those nuts shifting and even the jack can be an effort too at times.

She seemed very pleased to receive a helping hand but as she showed us to her boot and the spare wheel, all hopes were soon dashed as it quickly became apparent, she had no wheel brace or jack. Can't remember now if it was just one of these or both but either way the task was impossible without these basic essential tools.

She had a mobile and was in contact with someone else she knew so at least that made us feel a bit better. The fact it would soon be dropping dark really did put us in a bit of a dilemma as we didn't want to leave her stranded on her own, nor did we want to still be out walking the roads ourselves after dark. She was defiantly in touch with help on her phone, so we decided to press on.

As we did so, another car pulled up behind her in the layby. Did we go back and offer help once again as surely even if this new arrival couldn't change the wheel, there would be a high chance that they would be carrying the right tools which would allow us to do it for her. We decided between us that she would manage to get clear of trouble soon without our help.

I must admit I did feel a bit guilty and a bit pleased all at the same time. Pleased we'd stopped and tried to help out and in a weird sort of way pleased we weren't able to and guilty we hadn't turned back the second time when we probably could have assisted more. Mind if she knew the state of my feet, I'm sure she would have fully understood.

We needed to press on and press on we did. A few miles further ahead and we found ourselves on the single-track lanes again. Light was starting to fade and we still had several miles to go. For all we knew it was now country lanes all the way there and with distinct lack of street lights these lanes were sure to be pitch black in a short while.

My feet were starting to kill again but we had to just keep pushing. We seemed so near but so far away. Thanks for the weather being so fine that afternoon else night time would have crept up on us all the sooner.

We made it back to another main road and we were now heading directly towards the Inn. The road was fast moving, quite bendy and dam right dangerous in places and to be honest with the fading light upon us we were really desperate to complete today's task.

We were heading for the Premier Inn at Quintrell Downs. This wasn't the original planned stop but was a second choice after the other one was already fully booked. We were on the main road heading directly towards Newquay.

It wasn't just me that had had enough today, even Edd thought our journey seemed never ending as our destination seemed ever further away. It just seemed that every time we got round the next bend or deviation or over the next bump, we were expecting to see the end but it always appeared to still be a fair way up in the distance.

As the views changed, you could just about make out a settlement ahead but I'm sure it kept moving! It's amazing how long a mile can seem when you're tired and counting down the yards.

Surprisingly, a gentleman travelling on the other side of the road, going in our direction, stopped and offered us both a lift. Of course, I had to refuse! Can't remember now if he'd past us and turned round and came back or not but I do remember how surprised I was for somebody to stop.

You just don't expect that sort of thing when there are two of you. He was surely concerned about the dangerous road we were walking and the fact it was getting dark, as he expressed his concerns. We were very grateful for him for offering.

My legs were almost in his car but my head just wouldn't allow it. As we closed in on the last few hundred yards, we got a glimpse of the sea as the sun was setting down on the horizon. If I recall it was 9:15pm.

Our arrival at Quintrell Downs couldn't have come any sooner. What a day today had been. That was the last of my major hikes as tomorrow was a lot shorter being just over 20 miles.

Yet another evening sitting in the restaurant with my feet throbbing. No shoes on again and my legs up on the seat next to me. Not the best example to set in a restaurant but an unfortunate necessity.

I'm sure this was the evening we had one of the most miserable members of staff serve us, she really didn't want to be there and it wasn't just us she seemed to have an attitude with, she seemed to be completely unsociable with everyone.

We were one of the last if not the last in the restaurant that evening and I was quite pleased to get a smile out of her before we finished. She may of course just be glad her shift was over, who knows!

It's always hard to know what's really going on in somebody's head and sometimes in life we can be so quick to judge others. Sometimes, some people just need a bit more tolerance than others, for different reasons.

Personally, I think she was overworked as the place seemed understaffed and I think she was a bit peed off about it or maybe of course she'd just had a bad day. The problem is knowing when to complain about someone or not.

What I mean is how do you know that they're not just having a really tough time and the disciplinary action as a direct result of your complaint could be the last straw that pushes them over the edge?

Well just a thought! I held back a complaint about someone once for that very reason, then later learnt that no he's just a miserable sod all the time!

Well at least today was over, not that it left us much time to recover before getting up and starting all over again in the morning.

# Chapter 16
# A Boring Day!

Thursday 23$^{rd}$ June. A bit of an easier day today and what a relief. Next destination Camborne and tonight would be my last stay in a Premier Inn. Not really too much to say about today without boring you, so we'll try to keep it short and sweet.

Up and out early, feet still not in good shape so I spent a fair bit of time getting them wrapped as best as possible. Becoming a bit of an expert now at wrapping them up. Across the road before we set off for some essential supplies, I remember getting some fig rolls, silly things you remember, haven't eaten them for years until now; almost forgot they made them.

Always looking for snacks that gave you high energy release. Yesterday Edd was sharing out his mint cake, good for a quick sugar buzz. I must say Edd came pretty well prepared when it comes to things like that, must be all those years of camping I suppose. As Edd's bag was mainly full of food supplies, it was gradually getting lighter and lighter unlike mine.

We set off in great spirit, knowing we had a much shorter day and I suppose the end was now almost in sight, being the last but one day of hiking or limping in my case. Set off still heading towards Newquay before taking a left turn not too far up and passing a short section of roadworks on the way.

I do find it strange now when you look back, at some of the vivid recollections like small details like roadworks and even what we bought in certain shops as I was just mentioning. Anyway, as I said I shall try not to bore you with some of the smaller probably completely irrelevant details.

After taking this left turn at roundabout, we had to follow a major road, A3075, which I must admit seemed to go on for miles and miles and miles, it really did seem like a real boring part of the journey and unfortunately there was no alternative route either.

I do remember one of the breaks we took. We were sitting high up on a walled verge for a quick picnic, morning break or lunch, whatever you want to call it. It was an unusual verge with a small strip of grass along the roadside with a tall brick wall running alongside retaining another narrow grass strip, then another retaining wall further back.

Obviously, the ground was quite high on that side of the road. I still remember struggling to reach the top of the wall, launching my bag up first and then hauling myself up. I actually had to go a few yards along where the wall was slightly lower than walk back to where we wanted to perch.

I'm usually a bit more agile than that but my body was fair tired and weary, not to mention the soreness in places. It was great for a while having your feet completely suspended just dangling over the edge with no weight baring down on them but of course there's always a price to pay and the thought of jumping back down onto the ground below with my perishing feet was soon a reality. I'm sure my bag felt a lot heavier too!

Off we set again on what really seemed to be a long boring walk despite the fact it was a lot shorter than yesterday it still felt like a major chore. We eventually made it up and over a ridge at the top of the distant hill, crossing a big main road again, the A30 again, what a surprise!

We got back onto some much quieter roads and it wasn't long after passing a council worker cutting some nearby grass verges that our satnav decided to play a trick on us. By the way that wasn't the most efficient council or of course they could argue otherwise, the grass was about six foot high.

So, any way we started veering off this road and down an even quieter road. We get down so far only to be confronted with a disused gateway in a fence. When I say disused, I am assuming slightly, as beyond the fence appeared to be a footpath or what was once a footpath or right of way.

If you thought the grass cutting was a bit overdue, the footpath maintenance was pretty much non extinct. I don't think even a sickle would have been much help, possible a chainsaw was the only answer.

So very, very annoyingly we had to turn and back track back up this hill to the road where we'd forked off. The satnav here was trying to cut a short corner off our route but caused us to walk further thanks to the over enthusiastic council there. Shouldn't complain really because 99.5 % of the time it was so damn useful.

We were now close and heading in towards the town of Redruth. My feet were starting to give me real grief again as the cling film had displaced itself from its comfortable position and as I tried to resist stopping, it moved around and found its way between my toes and became un-walkable.

As it strangled my every step, I could have screamed at the discomfort. I had no choice but to stop again, strip my boots and socks and adjusted the film around my feet once again, just like I had done yesterday. At least today we were not under such a great time pressure and knowing this was my last but one trek, there was no way I could give up now.

Desperate to find a place to stop, we stopped at a junction and there on a grass verge lay a small wooden boat with two oars. I remember joking around with Edd about getting into the boat and taking a few snaps for a laugh, just like we'd taken a snap of me sitting on that road work vehicle near Exeter and the other on the back of that old truck at the saw mill. Didn't bother in the end.

There were so many photos we could have taken on route, so many I would have liked to have taken but most often than not, it was through pain and discomfort that stopped me bothering to do just that!

Feet more comfortable again we marched down in towards Redruth. Pretty little town that I remember, pedestrianised at its centre. The weather was nice the sun was shining and the town was bustling with people. I had one thing on my mind as we made it through and one thing only, I needed some more Sudocrem for my feet.

I spotted a shop it was either a Boots or a Super drug, can't remember now, think it was a Boots. Anyway, against Edd wishes, we had to stop again. I must admit he didn't complain once but I could see by his face that he'd rather press on than keep dragging it out as I were.

There was a bench in the middle of the high street. Edd parked himself down, so I decided I may as well offload my rucksack rather than traipse around the shop with it as it wasn't exactly easy navigating around a small shop with a huge bag protruding from your back.

It was great to get the weight off my back for a mo. The high street had quite a slope downwards, which I'd been managing quite fine with my stick until now but after offloading my luggage, all suddenly felt a bit weird. As I left Edd and wandered downwards over to the shop unladed, my legs suddenly felt all wobbly as I walked with no load.

It was a really strange feeling. My legs had got so used to taking the strain of the load going downhill but now the load was absent, my legs suddenly couldn't cope. Such a strange feeling, I'll never forget it.

Anyway, so I managed to get what I so desperately needed, got back to Edd, sat down and redid my feet properly. The Sudocrem was for later but I redid my feet again with the Vaseline. I remember an old lady sitting down nearby us, she started chatting to us and couldn't help remarking on my feet when she sees them.

*"You need to get them looked at!"*

She exclaimed to me, she sounded quite concerned. I knew my feet weren't in the best of shape but I wasn't overly concerned. As far as I was concerned, they just needed a damn good rest and that wasn't going to happen until I had completed this walk entirely! I'd now done about 300 miles and was still mentally determined to finish what I had started.

As we approached, Camborne you could see tall rise buildings in the distance that seemed to never get any closer or certainly seemed an age away. Our last few miles led us straight through a housing estate and it always felt like just round the next corner and we'd be there, despite the fact that Edd had the satnav telling us exactly what distance we had left to go.

I must admit, I may have already mentioned but not being in control of the satnav was not always easy for me. During the first six days when I was on my own, I would look at the satnav at the end of the journey a lot and literally count down the last few hundred yards. Now not having the satnav myself, as the week wore on, I found myself guessing the miles we had done and the miles left to go.

Unfortunately, as the miles got harder and harder, as best I tried to estimate in my head, the more and more disappointed I become with my guesstimating as we'd always done less than I thought, well most of the time anyway, despite trying to put myself into some kind of trance to ignore the pain. We made it to Camborne Premier Inn at a reasonable time. I must admit yet again the last few miles seemed endless.

We arrived at the Inn, feet throbbing as usual, tired, hungry but glad to have arrived a bit earlier than the previous evenings. My stomach had started to twinge a little from all the tablets I'd been taking. It wasn't until nearer the end of the walk that I actually realised that I'd actually been overdosing on the paracetamol on top of taking the ibuprofen. I had overlooked the maximum amount per day whoops!

It wasn't our finest stay I must say, so shame to say we didn't finish our Premier stay on a high. The restaurant in particular was extremely slow, poor service and understaffed. One thing I do remember was my starter being a dish of cold soup or should I say half a dish.

I suppose it would have been good to finish on an appraisal for Premier Inn being our last night with them but I can't say they ever did me any favours with helping out with the cost of my rooms, considering it was all for a good cause!

Well, 312 miles behind us and now only 23 miles stood between me and Land's End. At least my feet had more time to rest this evening, more time to recuperate before their final battle tomorrow. Somehow despite the state of my feet, I just had to find a way of completing my challenge even if it meant me doing the last few miles on my hands and knees.

# Chapter 17
# The Final Struggle

Friday 24<sup>th</sup> June. I'm sure you all remember where you were the morning of 24<sup>th</sup> June. It was the morning of the Brexit results. Last day today, last crazy day, only another 23miles to go and my mission would be complete. Destination Land's End. All sounds easy enough doesn't it, just a 23-mile stroll to the end of Cornwall.

Not too much to ask, one would think but add on the baggage I was carrying and the state of my feet and to be quite honest with you, I was barely fit enough to make it out of the front door after breakfast!

Mentally, I should have been on an enormous high knowing I was so close to completion but truth was I was in real doubt whether I could make it but somehow, just somehow, I had to!

Up early as usual, breakfast and out with a goal in mind, not just to complete today but also to reach Land's End by 6pm. Do you remember the radio show we talked about, well I promised Gary on Kennet radio that I would keep in touch and let him know when I arrived at Land's End, so it would be great if I could send him a message before his show ended.

We set off from the Inn, weather not too bad to start but a bit drizzle here and there which gradually got heavier and heavier and before long we both had to stop and cover up with our waterproofs before we got too much of a soaking. Didn't actually turn out too bad a day weather wise after that initial soaking.

The sky gradually broke as the sun rose higher and gave way too quite a pleasant day. As I said my feet weren't in the best of shape but regardless to this, I had decided to try a film free day today with no cream and a good thick pair of socks for added comfort.

The first few miles were a bit doggy with narrow country lanes and a few dodgy bends. This lane led us down to a large roundabout junction and there just before the junction was a large garage on the right-hand side. I never missed the opportunity for essential supplies so there I was again, off shopping while Edd guarded the entrance to the forecourt.

He always seemed so eager to keep going but had he had been with me since the start of the walk, then maybe things would have been a wee bit different. I know that even Edd had suffered a few blisters by this point but was showing a brave face. The condition of his feet wasn't perfect but far from the unbearable state of mine.

The pace of my walk in the first few days was just tad faster than now. When I say a tad, I was practically running at times. I was covering so much ground so quickly at times. I couldn't help wondering how Edd's feet would be right now had he been on his second week. Bear in mind of course, my feet weren't right from the word go!

Away from the roundabout and we were soon hiking a rather large, wide, fast-moving carriageway. Edd hadn't had to do too much of this since he'd met up with me. We'd been lucky the second week with miles and miles of country lanes to navigate.

This carriageway seemed to be a huge wide-open road in places and as it stretched out ahead of us it seemed to have a never-ending curve and gradient as it swung round to the right passing under what seemed like bridge after bridge. It wasn't actually a dual carriageway but was more than two lanes in places. I do believe now we were on the Halye bypass.

The choice of not wrapping up my feet today was a bad move and yet again, I just had to stop and sort them out again. They just seemed to be heating up and heating up as I marched on until they became intolerable again. So, we found a place to perch at the side of the carriageway and did what I could with the cling film and Vaseline to try to alleviate the pain of the constant friction.

All seemed much improved after that attention but to be totally honest with you, it was never perfect, never would be, I just had to accept my feet had simply had about all they could take. Every step was becoming a real effort regardless to how I walked, what pace, what angle or how I covered them up. Mt feet were really getting quite desperate!

As we neared the end of this carriageway which flowed down towards another large roundabout, the views were fantastic as the land ahead offer itself to the sea on both sides. Not only did we get a good glimpse of the sea but to see the coast addressing the land on both sides simultaneously gave us a real sense of how far down we were and a sense that Land's End was close beyond the distant horizon.

Wasn't time to get too excited knowing we had a good ten miles or so from Penzance and we still hadn't reached there yet. We could actually see Penzance in the distance to the south and the seafront felt like it was beckoning us onwards. Today's lunch view would be sitting down at the front, hopefully looking out at St Michael's Mount.

This would be our first proper brush with the coast since setting off. As we neared in towards Penzance, I remember passing a large flower plantation which I thought was unusual, you so often see fields of crops in this country but flowers not so commonly.

I couldn't wait to stop for lunch but my problem was sure to be getting going again. We soon closed in on the main road running alongside the sea front, where the only thing that stood between us and a great sea view was the railway line, the railway line we would be taking back home tomorrow.

We crossed over and headed for some steps that would take us up and over the tracks then straight onto the pavement along the front. I was literally counting down the last few paces as we crossed the bridge and headed for the first seat we could find. I was so content with the view.

Sitting there looking directly out at St Michael's Mount I felt a real sense of achievement. The fact I was now so near Land's End really did feel real. I can't remember now whether or not I removed my shoes that day, I think I just loosened my laces.

All I remember was how I sat there wondering how the hell I was going to carry on. My feet were literally throbbing and there's nothing I could do anymore to ease the pain. Even the weight of my feet dangling from the bench was more than I wanted to feel from them.

They were literally driving me mad which put me in a real dilemma, how the hell was I going to get through the next ten miles and on the other hand, how could I quit when I'd got so far and so close to the end? Quitting seemed so incomprehendible but almost reality at the same time.

I didn't want lunch to end that day but eventually of course it had to. Edd of course was keen to press on and I was quite sheepish in telling him just how much pain my feet were really in. We set off at a very slow pace, well Edd may have set off ahead of me and I had to catch up. The first few steps after stopping now always felt a bit torturous.

We had slightly deviated off course by crossing the railway line and going down onto the front itself so we had to wonder along and get ourselves back on route. We strolled along the front to the end of the railway track, past the station and back up into the town. As we made our way through the bustling town, I kept a keen eye out for a cash point.

Thinking ahead, we needed cash out as we were going to have to book a taxi back to Penzance to catch our train back home tomorrow. Walking back to Penzance tomorrow was certainly out of the question. So, cash all sorted and a last can of Red Bull and we were off. Hopefully this would be my last one, one last boost for the final push.

Looking back now, I still wonder how I made it that day. As we left Penzance in the distance behind us somehow my mind took over my body and just kept pushing, step by step by step. My feet were physically wrecked and in no fit state to carry on but somehow, I just kept going, almost like I was in some kind of mental trance not completely registering the pain I was feeling as I trudged on.

I do remember that last road being deadly in places. There were many places where the footpaths or even any kind of area to walk was just non-existent and there were crazy dangerous bends and racing vehicles including lorries.

As the road careered up and down and in and out towards Land's End these were amongst some of the worst bends, we'd had to endure the whole journey. Again, some of the drivers were quite aggressive, shouting and swearing at us despite the lack of footpaths.

Land's End seemed to get no nearer no matter how far we plodded on, in fact I'm sure it was getting further away! You'd see it in the distance constantly teasing you as the road swung one way then another. If I remember right even the signs were playing tricks on us with the mileage, I'm sure I remember one where the mileage had actually gone up!

I've been to Land's End before and remembered the big carpark you get to just before you arrive and was half expecting to see it every time, we turned the next bend but it just never came.

I had to stop numerous times during the final drag. Each stretch I managed to walk seemed to get shorter and shorter, almost getting to the point where I'd stop and a have a drink then do a few more hundred yards. Even Edd was beginning to feel the route was never ending, largely I guess due to my constant stopping and starting as we painfully pushed forward.

The final ten miles felt like twenty, the final mile felt like five and as I turned the last bend and dragged myself through the carpark, following the signs for the hotel and begging for them to take me the shortest route, all my mind could think of was it'll soon be over.

I was there! I'd made it! The only goal I had right now was to get through those hotel doors, into reception and plant myself in the first seat I could set my eyes on. The famous Land's End sign that everybody seems to associate with, that place was of no interest to me at this point.

All I needed to do was to get the weight off my feet and fast. I'd always had this vision in my mind that I would get to Land's End and throw my stick in the air in triumphant celebration but that just wasn't to be.

The strange thing was, I had no excitement that I'd made it, no celebrations, no emotions of pleasure or sense of achievement what so ever, just pure relief that it was all over. To be honest, I don't think the reality of what I'd just achieved had entered my head in the slightest.

One thing I do remember doing was sending a text to Gary at Kennet radio to let him know I had arrived. Amazingly, we had arrived at Land's End at about 5:45pm. Looking back at my phone, I'd texted Gary about 3:45pm to say we were about 5 miles away which means it took us two hours to do that last five miles. Two and a half miles an hour is not a good pace, even though it felt like we were really pushing it hard at times.

Edd checked in before me while I sat and rested for a bit. I pulled the boots from my feet and sat there for a good ten minutes doing nothing other than rehydrate myself and sort the paperwork out for my room. Great news, I was on the top floor!

Can't remember what room number it was now but it was up a few flights of stairs. One thing I do remember clearly mind was the lovely deep piled carpets that covered them. I slowly hobbled along and dragged myself up using my stick to ease the pressure on my feet, the deep piled carpet a real comfort to my painful soles.

Along the landing and into my room where my bed was calling for me to get my feet off the floor. Seemed a bit strange entering into such a small room but didn't think about it too long, only thing on my mind was to put my feet up, time to relax, time to heel at last, finally time for my damaged feet to start to mend. It was finally over!

I'd arranged to meet Edd downstairs a bit later that evening so I had a little while yet so I thought I'd sit back and relax for a mo. Wasn't that long in fact, in fact I'd barely set my arse down before my phone started bleeping. It was a text from another old customer of mine, Alan and Carol Brindley.

*"Where are you?"* They asked.

*"At Land's End,"* I replied.

*"I've just made it here, just arrived!"* Then came the reply.

*"So are we!"* Believe it or not that they were actually very close by. In fact, when they explained where they were, I couldn't believe when I looked down outside the hotel, they were virtually under my window! I had a couple of Stalkers, all the way down to Land's End I'd gone and I had a couple of bloody stalkers!

I was so surprised to hear from them, I asked them to meet me in the hotel lobby at the bottom of the stairs. I made my way back down to them, at least this time I didn't need to drag my bag along with us or boots even, just me and my sore feet hobbling back down on this lovely deep piled carpet.

Despite having to drag myself back down again, it was really great to see them both, not to mention unexpected! We had a bit of a chat and they got to see my feet, mind not too sure if they really appreciated that but it was the least, I could do to show them how much effort I'd put in.

As it turned out I was very, very grateful to them as they very kindly offered to come back the next morning and give both me and my mate a lift back to Penzance. They were apparently staying at a hotel just along the coast somewhere if I remember rightly.

They didn't want to keep me too long; I'm sure my face said it all if my feet didn't or the other way round? So, I said goodbye to them both and got back up to my room.

Back up to my room and I couldn't wait to freshen up and have a bath. My room was very quickly a complete mess where I'd came in the room and dumped stuff from my bag chaotically all over the floor to get to the bits I needed.

My feet were still throbbing and extremely sore and I could feel my stomach twinging from all the tablets I'd been taking. My little room had an on suite which was just as well as when I removed my socks from my feet, I'd lost so much skin from the bottom of my feet they were stinging, stinging so badly I had to walk on my hands and knees to the bathroom.

It might sound a bit crazy now but it was the truth. I had a nice deep bath then crawled back into my room on my hands and knees before smothering them in cream again and then covering them up, so I could go down for dinner.

I hobbled down to dinner again in my socks and with the aid of my stick and kept my walking to a bare minimum. I even asked them for a table not too far away. It was a lovely dining room and the food was great too.

I still remember sitting there gazing out to sea through the glass fronted wall that run the entire length of the restaurant. I relaxed as best I could, can't say I completely relaxed as my feet were constantly nagging during the whole course of my meal.

It was of course at last time to celebrate with a pint. Until now I hadn't been tempted with a single drink since I'd set out from London 12 days ago. Not too sure I should have been drinking with all those pills rattling around inside me but I did regardless, maybe in the hope it would numb the pain.

I don't know but I'd put myself through so much pain and agony that nothing was going to stop me having a few relaxing pints to see it all behind us!

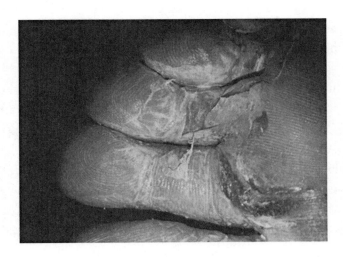

Seemed such a shame to be all the way down there at Land's End but not fit enough to be able to take a stroll around outside and appreciate the sheer beauty of rugged natural landscape and in particular the peace and tranquillity now most visitors had gone off home.

Unfortunately, the only place I was heading after my meal was back up to my room to put my feet up. I didn't find out until the next morning that Edd had gone back out and walked up the coast a bit which I didn't blame him, in fact I was probably a bit jealous.

Anyway, so I got back up to my room, straightened things out a bit for the morning, then watched a bit of TV. Can't say that really bother me much at the best of times so I ended up switching over to a music channel for a while. I also had the window fully open and lay their listening to the sea as it hammered itself against the coast line below.

I must have had the music on low till about 1 o'clock in the morning as I just couldn't settle down. I was trying my best not to take any more painkiller but as the last ones wore off, my feet were literally driving me mad to the point where I eventually gave in, just to be able to get a few hours' sleep; else I would have been completely knackered the next day.

It really did seem like a long night, mind not sure if that's the right way to describe it, no sooner the sun is set, it's showing its face again as it rises so early in the morning that time of year!

# Chapter 18
# A Few Pints Later!

Saturday 25<sup>th</sup> June. Up early, not that we were in any rush today whatsoever. Hadn't arranged to meet Edd for breakfast until about 9:15am, so a bit of a lazy start, we'd earned it. I had my bag all sorted and decided to go down and out the front for some fresh sea air. Bit of an outdoor man anyway so I really enjoyed sitting there for bit before breakfast.

Brekkie was great, in fact I must go back there one day for a second stay, then hopefully I can enjoy the hotel a bit more and appreciate its fantastic surroundings, especially the peace and tranquillity of the place as the evening comes to a close.

Anyway, so once brekkie was over, it was finally time to get my picture by the famous Land's End post. My feet were extremely sore, so I made my way down to the post at a snail's pace anxious to get my photo done but what I wasn't expecting when I got there was for it to be barred off by metal railings, only to be told if I wanted to get right up to it, I would have to pay.

I couldn't believe it, when I explained to the guy it was for a charity, he still demanded money off me, how sad was that, it wasn't like I was making it up, I even had the *'make a wish'* t-shirt on. To make things worse, he then tried to excuse himself by explaining that people came there to him on a daily basis, all supporting their different charities and he still demanded money off them all.

Well, what a complete saddo! Just a completely and utterly unscrupulous being if you ask me, how low can people really stoop? Shame on him! I refused to pay on principle and done the next best thing and got Edd to take a picture of me sitting on the metal railings with the post directly behind me.

Had I gone there the evening before, I could have walked right up to it but unfortunately with my feet being so sore, it was the last thing on my mind.

Alan and Carol weren't picking us up for a while, so we had some time to kill. Staying in the Land's End Hotel entitled us to free entrance into all the attractions there, so Edd went off for a quick look around while I confined myself to the nearest bench and awaited the opening of a coffee shop to grab a quick drink.

Alan and Carol picked us up as arranged. I had texted then to let them know we were ready earlier but I don't think they'd received the text. Didn't really want to bother them too much as it was so good of them to put themselves out to give us a lift in the first place. When they arrived, they met Edd for the first time. I made sure we took a quick opportunity to get a few snaps of us all together before we set off.

Travelling back to Penzance was a bit of an eye opener. It gave us a real sense of just how far we'd walked in pain the day before and just how damn dangerous some of those bends were. They dropped us off right near the station. There happened to be some kind of event going on in the town that day, so it was heaving with people.

After thanking them both and saying our goodbyes, we headed straight for one of the nearest pubs, close by to the station. The pub was also heaving with people as there was a match on, can't remember now if it was rugby or football.

We sank a few beers in there and managed to squeeze in another pub very close by before making our way over towards the station, ready to board our awaiting train.

I asked one of the platform guards to take a couple of snaps of me and Edd at the front on the train before boarding and finding our seats.

The first thing I did once we were seated on the train was to rip those boots from my feet for the final time. My feet were still in a fair bit of pain but all I could do was to grin and bear it, knowing that the best thing in the world now for them was just time and rest.

Our journey home seemed to go on forever. I guess I was just anxious to get home now and I must admit I was really, really looking forward to seeing Ann and the boys that day. That's the longest I've ever been away from my family but I guess my mind had just been so occupied with the pure determination and completion of what turned out to be a very trying task.

I enjoyed crossing over the Tamer Bridge on the way back and managed to get a great snap of it on the phone on my way past. Town after town, county after county, you suddenly started to get a real feel for just how far we'd actually walked.

To be quite honest I don't think the reality ever did sink in properly, as I said before when I arrived at Land's End I recall no happy moments of achievement, just relief it was all over. It's only when I look back now, I'm starting to see it as a sense of achievement.

Arrived at reading with Edd where we both went our separate ways. Edd had to change trains and carry on heading east whereas I had to change trains and head back west towards Newbury. My train was delayed, how unusual. I sat there on the platform, reading in my socks, bag by one side and boots by the other.

There was no way my boots were going back on my feet not even if somebody begged me or offered me a million dollars. I sat there on the platform and spoke to Annie and the boys while I was waiting.

Caught my train back to Newbury and couldn't wait to get back home. Walked out of Newbury station still in my socks and knew exactly where I was heading, I had no choice but straight to the nearest awaiting taxi. A big taxi it was, one of those MPV type vehicles.

I crawled up into the taxi, it seemed so much space for just me, well me, my big bag, stick and a pair of boots. Always seems strange for me to be in the back of a car, let alone a huge space with no one around me and someone else driving. I'd now not driven for a whole two weeks, that's got to be a record for me.

Got chatting a bit to the taxi driver on my short journey home. I'm sure the driver was wondering why I was in my socks. Very nice chap, he was easy to chat to, I know what you're thinking, he's a cabbie, so he would be easy to chat to but that's not always the case.

I tell you what over the years I've met many tradesmen, self-employed tradesmen that are right miserable sods and it just makes you wonder how they manage to keep employed as surely, they're relying on people recommending them on.

If I were a customer and I met a tradesman as grumpy as some of the ones I've had the pleasure or not so pleasure of crossing paths with, I certainly wouldn't be too keen to pass their details on even if they did do the right job!

Anyway, so we arrive home, I jump out the cab, well stumble out, went for my pocket to get some cash out to pay my fare and this guy says:

*"No that's ok sir, this one's on me."*

Well, I was quite taken back, I surely wasn't expecting this. Then to top this off even further, he went into his own pocket, pulled out a tenner and handed it over to me.

*"Here's a small contribution to your charity."*

I was gob smacked! I just wasn't expecting it, I suppose. I guess you try so hard trying to raise money sometimes that when it comes to you unexpectedly without any request what so ever it's such a delight. I think what really made it feel so special was that this was the final moment of my walk and it had finished on such a high.

So, whoever you are if you're reading this, I'd like to thank you for your kindness. Can't say I'm good with faces plus my mind was on other things that day so I probably wouldn't recognise you if I bumped into you again but you know who you are and you made my day!

So good to see the family again. Spent the next few days hobbling round on my stick. Couldn't even sleep with the bed covers over my toes. Surprise, surprise! Monday morning, I was on the phone making an appointment with a doctor.

Despite the rest, my left foot had become very warm and swollen up. Neither of my feet were that good, so I ended up on antibiotics as they were infected where I'd lost so much skin from walking so badly on them.

Also had to take the next full week off work to allow then to heel a bit. Believe it or not, it was actually several months on from that day until my feet felt anywhere near right again. For a long time, I couldn't stand comfortably on hard concrete for any real period of time.

Hard to describe but my feet just felt hypersensitive as if the skin was wafer thin and all-natural cushioning removed. When you think about the weight of your body, it's amazing really what your feet go through, how we simply take them for granted but hey! Don't we just do that with so many things in life!

# Chapter 19
## On Reflection

Looking back now, I am really glad I decided to do it. It's strange sometimes how such tiny things we do in life can take us on such huge journeys, even change your life completely as one small thing leads to another. We go through life making small changes, often taking small chances of little significance but each often having a small effect on the next without even realising.

Maybe it was the first job you had or the first friend you had or maybe the first time you stood up for yourself and it moulds us, the way we think, what we do next and so on. In the same way, we could also consider what we haven't done in life, what might have been had we chosen slightly different paths here and there and where we might have been now?

I've never been one for over reflecting on the past but this whole walk, this whole idea, was all from one spur of the moment thought in my head, a sudden urge or a passion to do something one day!

One thing I didn't realise was the sheer amount of time this whole thing was about to zap up from my life, the walking, the training, the organising and the fundraising. I learnt so much about people. You can sometimes empty a room by asking people to stick their hands in their pockets for nothing in return and that's nothing to do with the money people do or don't have.

Some are so generous beyond comparison and it's all about the simple nature of people. Be it kindness, sympathy, greed, selfishness, selflessness, ego, heartfelt, heartless, self-indulgent, everybody having different values about life and all around them. I must admit I was completely surprised by some of the reactions I had from others, yet some people just blew me away!

Then of course, there was all the training or lack of. Just how do you train for something like that without spending hours and hours walking? I just don't know. Would I do something like that again?

Well, all I can say is I wouldn't completely rule it out but I'd have to really consider just how dangerous some of that walk really was! With the sheer absence of footpaths, it really was like playing Russian roulette with the motorists at times.

The highlights for me were without doubt some of the wonderful people I met on my way and even before I set off. And of course, just being out all the time, that's one thing I really did enjoy!

When I think of it sometimes, it does seem like a great achievement but when you look at what some other people do for charities it also seems so trivial, almost like making a fuss of something unworthy of such complaints. I guess what made all the difference was the state my feet were in before I actually set off.

When I think of it like that, I did actually complete the walk against all odds. I had a damaged left ankle, a probable broken little toe on my right foot and sore skin on both heels.

The knock-on effect from this saw me limping the majority of the distance and losing a lot of skin off the bottom of my feet including losing a second toe nail completely still attached to a big lump of skin as it peeled away from my toes on my left foot! Because I had to keep on target every day I just had to keep going, I couldn't stop until I reached my destination.

I could have quit at any stage but I just couldn't bring myself round to doing that. I still don't know how the hell I managed to do that last ten miles to Land's End. I could barely stand on my feet when I got there! It really must have been a case of mind over matter, so I've learnt a lot about myself as well with my self-determination and refusing to quit.

I've always been a very self-motivated person; hence my walk was my route, my dates, my distance and my way but I'll always be so grateful to my fantastic friend Eddie for joining me along the way. Memories I'll have forever. Memories I'll always cherish!

Lastly, I'd like to thank you for taking the time to read my story. Writing this book has also been a great sense of achievement for me. I only hope you enjoyed it and I'd like to thank you for all your support as 90% of any profits from this book goes directly to charity.

I wish you all the very best!